GOD

AT WORK
IN
SAINTS OF OLD

Come and see the **works of God:**
He is **awesome** in His doing
toward the sons of men.
Psalm 66:5, NKJ

GOD
AT WORK
IN
SAINTS OF OLD

Ervin N. Hershberger

Distributed by:
CHOICE BOOKS OF NORTHERN VIRGINIA
P.O. Box 4080
Manassas, VA 20108
We Welcome Your Response

ISBN: 0-9717054-3-7

Unless otherwise noted all Scripture references are
from the **King James Version** of the Holy Bible.

Published by Vision Publishers
Harrisonburg, Virginia

Cover Design: Lonnie D. Yoder

For additional copies or comments write to:
Vision Publishers
P.O. Box 190
Harrisonburg, VA 22803
or Fax 1-540-432-6530
(see order forms in back)

Anyone wishing to write the author may do so at:
732 Saint Paul Road
Meyersdale, PA 15552
Phone: 814-662-2483
email: enhershberger@cs.com

Dedication

I dedicate this book
to the Holy Trinity,
Father, Son, and Holy Spirit,
each working faithfully in His specific role,
yet also working in perfect unity,
for and with fallen man.

Contents

Credits Due

To the lasting memories of my departed wife, whose loving companionship for more than 60 years sustained and encouraged me to the very end of her pilgrimage.

To Marvin and Mildred Yoder (son-in-law and daughter) for critiquing my manuscripts and giving much help and many valuable suggestions.

To friends, too numerous to name herein, for their prayers, friendship, and encouragement in many ways.

To Vision Publishers for finalizing the project, formatting, printing, publishing, and marketing the book.

May God Almighty, who was truly at work in saints of old, be glorified with whatever He chooses to do with the messages in this book. He alone can make these pages fruitful for His glory and for the good of mankind.

Introduction

Reading this book reminded me of the encouraging and comforting hymn:

> *"God moves in a mysterious way, His wonders to perform:*
>
> *He plants His footsteps in the sea, and rides upon the storm."*

In *God at Work in Saints of Old*, the author walks the reader through the Scriptures and highlights some of the ordinary people God used in fulfilling His plan to offer spiritual salvation to fallen mankind. It not only shows how God used ordinary people in extraordinary ways, but how ordinary people who placed their faith in an extraordinary God became part of the great wonders of the works of God.

On these pages we are introduced to Abraham, known as a man of faith. He was also an ordinary man subject to failure and yet "proved his loyalty and total obedience to God." Then we read of Jacob who was "inclined toward bargains, not brothers," and Esau whose "spirit of revenge drained out of him." It is very interesting to read of Joseph and how God worked wonders in his life as a "human foreshadow of Jesus Christ." It is noteworthy to see what "God wrought through the simple, trusting faith" of Moses' parents. Then there is a section on how God worked wonders through four women mentioned in the Bible. And as one would expect in a book like this, there is the account of David with "an unshakable faith in God." Attention is also drawn to God using pagan kings to bring about His will. It is encouraging to read the account of four Jewish slaves who resisted the extreme peer pressure of the pagan king, and of Daniel who survived international revolutions and the fierce lions' den. One should not miss the account of Mary, the maiden of faith, who became a mother of fame, whose name continues to circle the earth with millions of namesakes.

Throughout the Bible we see accounts of how God worked through ordinary people who submitted their lives to Him. Many of their accounts are accompanied by failures, disappointments, and bitter tastes. However, because of their faith in the extraordinary God, He still works wonders through their lives.

The hymn again comes to mind:

"His purposes will ripen fast, unfolding every hour.
The bud may have a bitter taste, but sweet will be the
flow'r."

This book is a reminder that every person is precious in the sight of God, and every true believer of Jesus Christ has a work to do. Christians are ordinary people who serve an extraordinary God who still works wonders through His children today.

Here is some enriching reading for seeking souls who want to grow in the grace and knowledge of our Lord and Savior, Jesus Christ.

Simon Schrock
June 2002

Preface

Men and angels are the only creatures created as free moral agents. They alone are capable of intelligent communion and cooperation with God, or of resisting the will of God. Therefore both men and angels are always accountable to God for their conduct, and for the intents of their hearts. Animals are controlled and regulated by instinct, rather than by responsible intellect. Inanimate things, like stars and planets, are controlled solely by the mind and will of God, embodied in the natural laws that He has established. Therefore they **never malfunction**.

However, the time is coming when He will replace this marvelous system with something even better, more wonderful, and everlasting. *"Heaven and earth shall pass away, but my words shall not pass away"* (Matthew 24:35). *"For, behold, I create new heavens and a new earth: and the former shall not be remembered, nor come into mind"* (Isaiah 65:17). The Bible also shows that whoever and whatever has ignored and resisted His will for ages will then be completely subdued and brought under His control.

God has not left man to himself, unaided by divine assistance, nor to do as he pleases. He keeps in touch, and seeks personal fellowship with every individual to give guidance, direction, and enablement. But He expects us to seek and to serve Him willingly by choice. If we choose otherwise, He may discipline us to bring us back to Himself. But if we resent His loving discipline, He may let us go our own way, all the way to total ruin. That *"God loveth a **cheerful** giver"* is not limited to monetary giving. He wants hearts that are willingly and cheerfully given to Him.

From Genesis through The Revelation we see God at work in fallen and failing vessels of clay, especially after they submitted themselves to Him. In this book we are seeking to learn from the lives of people whose record God preserved for our learning and instruction. The list is selective for the sake of brevity, and by no means exhaustive. Others, especially the prophets, offer a great deal of important information that God wants all of us to know.

Books like this are supplemental, encouraging study of the Bible, which is God's message printed out for man. We recommend a thorough study of the basics straight from the Bible, by which all manmade books must be tested.

God, in preparing His people for eternal bliss, keeps testing and **proving** us for the express purpose of **improving** our blessedness. That, in a general way, is true of all people. It is true in a special way of His chosen people Israel[1] and of His Church, the body of Christ.[2] No one can improve on what God has done, is doing, and finally will do.

1. Exodus 19:5; Deuteronomy 7:6; 14:2; 26:17-19; 1 Kings 8:53; Psalm 33:12; 135:4; Isaiah 66:22; Jeremiah 46:28.

2. Matthew 16:18; Acts 20:28; Romans 5:6, 8, 10; 12:5; Ephesians 1:23; 3:9, 10; 4:11-13; 5:25-27; 1 Peter 2:9, 10.

—Ervin Hershberger

1

The Blessedness of Accountability

*And the L*ORD *God took the man, and put him into the garden of Eden **to dress it and to keep it**. . . . But of the tree of the knowledge of good and evil, **thou shalt not eat of it:** for in the day that thou eatest thereof thou shalt surely die.*
(Genesis 2:15, 17)

Accountability, a Universal Principle

God did not make human puppets. He created intelligent people, capable of willing obedience, able to follow instructions and to make wise choices. Fresh from the hand and breath of God, they were pure and holy, perfect in every way. They were not God's equal but His subjects, therefore always fully accountable to Him. That applies to every human being on earth, for we are all descendants of Adam and Eve by birth.

God had planted a beautiful garden where the atmosphere, environment, and climate were perfect for both physical comfort and the production of fruit, vegetables, and herbs. In the midst of that garden He had put the tree of the knowledge of good and evil, apparently for the express purpose of helping man to develop the imperative virtues of subordination, accountability, and obedience. "And God saw every thing that he had made, and, behold, it was very good."

Adam and Eve enjoyed the most wonderful fellowship with God. To them, accountability was far superior to any service manual. Whenever God *visited* with them in the garden, they could discuss every activity and every plan directly with the Creator. Talk about solving problems—they had it made! Their willing dependence upon His loving care naturally made His instructions, protective commandments, and loving corrections a most pleasant experience.

That virtually collapsed when Satan invaded the Garden of Eden and beguiled Eve (Genesis 3:1-6). He persuaded her to believe that eating the forbidden fruit would make them wise, **like God** in their own right, apart from God. She listened—looked—lusted—and finally took and ate.

Adam was not deceived,[1] nevertheless, he joined Eve in the transgression in spite of better knowledge. Their eyes indeed were opened, but it brought death to the human race. For by that act *"sin entered into the world, and death by sin; and so death passed upon all men, for that all have sinned"* (Romans 5:12b). To assume independence from or equality with God spells death to mortal man, and so it was for them. For the first time they were afraid to give an account of their activities that day. In fact, they were afraid of God and tried to hide.

Adam, as head of the human race, is the figure of him that was to come (Romans 5:14), namely Jesus Christ. *"For if by one man's offence death reigned by one [Adam]; much more they which receive abundance of grace ... shall reign in life by one, Jesus Christ"* (Romans 5:17). Just as every human being ever born on earth is the offspring and heir of Adam, even so every soul that is saved is a trophy of the redemptive work of Jesus Christ. In Christ, the blessing of always being accountable can be restored to every true believer.

Self-expression, a Universal Problem

Cain also despised accountability and dared to tempt God with a bloodless offering,[2] which he evidently knew was not what God desired. Then he was jealous because Abel's lamb was accepted and angry because his own fruit of the ground did not suffice. In anger, he killed his righteous brother and lied to God about his sin. Instead of repenting when God pled with him, he only groaned about the severity of his punishment and *"went out from the presence of the* LORD.*"*

Cain, being the *first birth* on record, typifies us in our *first birth*. First, we are born of flesh and with a sinful nature inherited from Adam. Therefore, we all need a second birth. *"Except a man be born again, he cannot see the kingdom of God"* (John 3:3b). Our second birth is *"not of blood, nor of the will of the flesh, nor of the will of man, but of God"* (John 1:13b). Cain typifies those who refuse to acknowledge and confess their sin. They reject God's ample provision for salvation, and going out from the presence of God they perish in self-destruction.

Five generations later that same rebellious spirit welled up in Lamech, one of Cain's descendants. He also spurned his accountability to God, and boasted to his wives that he had slain a man. We can almost see him clenching his fist and flexing his muscles, saying, *"If Cain shall be avenged sevenfold, truly Lamech seventy and sevenfold."*[3] There, in the seventh generation, the Biblical record of Cain's family ends with the boastful threats of a murderer.[4] His surviving descendants all died in the Flood. Subordination and accountability remained inevitable; but for them the blessing was replaced with a curse.

Accountability Is God's Safety Zone

Abel's works are acknowledged as righteous[5] because he sensed his need of atonement by the shedding of blood. That is why he offered a lamb as a sacrifice, and he offered it by faith, *"by which he obtained witness that he was righteous"* (Hebrews 11:4).

God's instructions are always safe and accurate. Violations thereof often played havoc even among

God's chosen people. In the Pentateuch alone Israel was warned five times not to provoke God (Exodus 23:21; Deuteronomy 4:25; 9:18; 31:20, 29), and nine times we find that they did provoke Him (Numbers 14:11, 23; 16:30; Deuteronomy 9:8, 22; 32:16, 19, 21). That is what the writer to the Hebrews calls *"the provocation"* (Hebrews 3:8), and solemnly warns us to beware of it. He was keenly aware that unbelieving scribes and Pharisees, yea, even the Sanhedrin that sentenced Jesus to die, had fallen into that very trap. His concern was that the Jews in His day (and we in our day!) should live accountably with respect and obedience.

Cooperation with God, by the grace of God and to the glory of God, brings the highest degree of bliss man can know in this life. But unregenerate man is inclined to resent accountability. He despises God-given restrictions. He wants to make his own rules, do his own thing, in his own way, by his own strength, and for his own glory. To assume we can be **like God** (self-sufficient in competition with God) is fatal conceit. Only self-centered conceit refuses accountability.

By faith in Christ, man can enjoy the blessing of daily laying his account open before God for auditing, correction, and redirection. That way we can enjoy the blessing of accountable fellowship with God, and by faith in His pardoning, sanctifying grace, inherit eternal life.

Questions for Consideration and Discussion

1. Before the fall, what made God's visits so pleasant?
2. Why did the serpent beguile Eve instead of Adam?
3. Why did sin enter "by one **man**" instead of by the woman?
4. How was Adam's sin different from the sin of Eve?
5. By what was Abel acknowledged righteous?
6. What can Christ's blood say that Abel's could not say (Hebrews 12:24)?
7. How did Cain's error advance into progressive sinning?
8. How did God wink at the time of ignorance (Acts 17:30)?
9. Why are we more accountable than Old Testament saints were?
10. What advantages do we have that they did not have?

---

1. 1 Timothy 2:14
2. Genesis 4:3-16
3. Genesis 4:23, 24
4. Genesis 4:24
5. 1 John 3:12

2

Walking With God
Assures Safety

The Biblical record after the seventh generation from Adam is confined to the descendants of Seth. We are spared the pain of seeing the corruption among the compromising majority of the sons of Adam. In this chapter we have the pleasure of observing the two men who the Bible says "walked with God." Both found perfect safety in so doing.

I. Enoch Walked With God

And Enoch walked with God: and he was not; for God took him (Genesis 5:24).

The Old Testament abounds with types and figures that foreshadow God's ultimate plans for mankind. Enoch's biography is very brief, saying nothing about any great deeds he had done. But the fact that he walked with God is stated twice. That reveals a relationship of explicit trust and confidence in God. It is a demonstration of salvation **by faith**, not of works: a doctrine that is clearly spelled out in the New Testament.

*By faith Enoch was translated that he should not see death; and was not found, because God had translated him: for before his translation he had this testimony, that he pleased God. But **without faith** it is impossible to please him: for he that cometh to God must believe that he is, and that he is a rewarder of them that diligently seek him (Hebrews 11:5, 6).*

Because Enoch walked with God by faith, God took him home without dying. Because he had such a close walk with the "Uppertaker," he never needed an undertaker.

Secondly, Enoch's unusual flight to heaven (in the seventh generation of mankind) beautifully foreshadows the *imminence* of the rapture. Imminence means it can happen at any moment, without any further notice. It was a preview of how Christians, who **by faith** have *"put their trust in Him"* (Psalm 2:12b), will some day *"be caught up . . . to meet the Lord in the air: and so shall we ever be with the Lord"* (1 Thessalonians 4:15-**17**).

By faith we *"look for the Saviour"* (Philippians 3:20b). **By faith** we *"wait for his Son from heaven"* (1 Thessalonians 1:10b). **By faith** we *"love his appearing"* (2 Timothy 4:8b). **By faith** we fondly anticipate the rapture, assured of going *home* with Him who so graciously took Enoch home to Himself. The compromising majority live by *flesh*, not by *faith*. As it was in the days of Enoch, so it is today.

II. Noah Walked With God

Noah was a great-grandson of Enoch, and the tenth generation of mankind. By his five hundredth year, the wickedness of man was great *"and the* L*ORD* *said, I will destroy man . . . from the face of the earth; . . . But Noah found grace in the eyes of the* L*ORD . . . [being] a just man and perfect in his generations, and Noah walked with God"* (Genesis 6:7-9).

Though Noah was *"a just man and perfect,"* he was saved **by the grace of God.** He had been born with a sinful nature, like everyone else. He too needed atonement, which he received by grace through faith. His "perfection" was not his personal accomplishment, but was accomplished **by God's grace through Noah's faith in the promises of God.**

> *By faith Noah, being warned of God of things not seen as yet, moved with fear, prepared an ark to the saving of his house; by the which he condemned the world, and became heir of **the righteousness which is by faith** (Hebrews 11:7).*

God Himself designed all the details. Nothing was left to Noah's ingenuity except to carry out precise instructions. The ark was made of gopher wood, **three** stories high, four hundred fifty feet long, seventy-five feet wide, and forty-five feet high, sealed with **pitch** inside and outside, with rooms and nests, one window at the top and **one door** in the side.

Evidently the people in Noah's day had never seen rain (Genesis 2:5, 6). When God told Noah to build the ark because He was going to destroy the earth with a flood,[1] the people did not believe Him. Imagine the ridicule Noah must have suffered from those unbelieving people who knew nothing of rain. To them that big boat was sheer folly—the laughing stock of the world. But Noah obeyed God, and kept right on building. His faith was bigger than the boat.

Noah is acknowledged as *"a preacher of righteousness"* (2 Peter 2:5), but his messages fell on deaf ears. Few people care to identify with a man who invests his life and savings in what they consider as a hopeless project. According to Adam Clarke's chronological chart the Flood came 669 years after Enoch was taken to heaven; five years after Noah's father, Lamech, had died; and the same year in which his grandfather, Methuselah, died. Poor Noah! If he had converts beyond his own family, they must have died before the rains came. Preaching to people who will not hear is extremely difficult.

> *And the LORD said unto Noah, Come thou and all thy house into the ark; for thee have I seen righteous before me in this generation. . . . For yet seven days, and I will cause it to rain upon the earth forty days and forty nights; and every living substance that I have made will I destroy from off the face of the earth. . . . And it came to pass after seven days, that the waters of the flood were upon the earth (Genesis 7:1, 4, 10).*

Noah and his family of eight people entered the

ark and waited. Unbelieving neighbors may have laughed them to scorn. Both beasts and fowl *"went in unto Noah into the ark, two and two of all flesh, wherein is the breath of life"* (Genesis 7:15). We read nothing of Noah rounding them up or driving them in. God moved the animals by instinct. But men, whose choices determine their destiny, refused to take warning even when they saw the animals enter the ark. The door was kept open for seven days, but not one more soul accepted the invitation. God never forces salvation upon an unwilling soul. After seven days God Himself shut the door—a right which He reserves for Himself.

> *In the six hundredth year of Noah's life, in the second month, the seventeenth day of the month, the same day were all the fountains of the great deep broken up, and the windows of heaven were opened. And the rain was upon the earth forty days and forty nights (Genesis 7:11, 12).*

> *And the waters prevailed exceedingly upon the earth; and all the high hills, that* were *under the whole heaven, were covered. . . . And every living substance was destroyed which was upon the face of the ground, both man, and cattle, and the creeping things, and the fowl of the heaven; and they were destroyed from the earth: and Noah only remained* alive, *and they that* were *with him in the ark (Genesis 7:19, 23).*

The universal death sentence could not be reversed, but God's grace provided a way for believers to rise above it. Not one soul perished in Noah's ark. It mattered not how heavy the torrent, how furious the tempest, nor how deep the waters; the ark rose triumphantly above it all. Like Christ, the ark safely kept everyone who abode within, but all who scoffed at the open door perished when the door was shut.

God judged that wicked and rebellious world with a universal Flood. The Ark was the only means of escape from death. Even so now, Jesus Christ is the absolute—but only—means of escape from the universal and fiery judgment of God in His final settlement with rebellious sinners.

> But the fearful, and unbelieving, and the abominable, and murderers, and whoremongers, and sorcerers, and idolaters, and all liars, shall have their part in the lake which burneth with fire and brimstone: which is the **second death** (Revelation 21:8).

> The same shall drink of the wine of the wrath of God, which is poured out without mixture into the cup of his indignation; and he shall be tormented with fire and brimstone in the presence of the holy angels, and in the presence of the Lamb (Revelation 14:10).

At this writing, Heaven's door is still open. God is still waiting. And *"we are ambassadors for Christ, as though God did beseech you by us: we pray you in Christ's stead, be ye reconciled to God"* (2 Corinthians 5:20). Today is the accepted time. Tomorrow may be too late.

Questions for Consideration and Discussion

1. What wonders did God do in Enoch's life?
2. What virtue of Enoch is an imperative for us?
3. What is typified by Enoch being taken without dying?
4. Of what, and of Whom, is the Ark a type?
5. Whom do Noah and his family in the Ark typify?
6. What is symbolized by **one opening in the side**?
7. Study the Hebrew word translated pitch (Genesis 6:14).
8. How did Noah become an heir of righteousness?
9. Would he have been spared without obedience in building?
10. What is typified by the Ark landing on the 17th of Abib (Genesis 8:4)?

---

1. Genesis 6:13-22

3

One Whom Satan Could Not Crush

*And the L*ORD *said unto Satan,*
Hast thou considered my servant Job, . . .
(Job 1:8a; 2:3a).

I. Satan, the Source of Suffering

Job, the oldest book in the Bible, shows what a man of God can endure by faith. Job lived long before the Bible was written, probably contemporary with Abraham. God described him as *"perfect* [by virtue of his faith] *and upright, and one that feared God, and eschewed evil."*[1] God used Job as a living demonstration of Heaven's power in a mortal man.

When the sons of God (holy angels) presented themselves before the LORD, Satan (an apostate angel) also came. God invited Satan to consider this outstanding man, Job.

> *And the L*ORD *said unto Satan, Hast thou considered my servant Job, that there is none like him in the earth, a perfect and an upright man, one that feareth God, and escheweth evil? (Job 1:8).*

Then Satan answered the L<small>ORD</small>, *and said, Doth Job fear God for nought? Hast not thou made an hedge about him, and about his house, and about all that he hath on every side? thou hast blessed the work of his hands, and his substance is increased in the land. But put forth thine hand now, and touch all that he hath, and he will curse thee to thy face (Job 1:9-11).*

And the L<small>ORD</small> *said unto Satan, Behold, all that he hath is in thy power;* **only upon himself put not forth thine hand.** *So Satan went forth from the presence of the* L<small>ORD</small> *(Job 1:12).*

God accepted Satan's challenge, knowing that Job would faithfully demonstrate divine keeping power even if Satan destroyed everything he owned. As soon as Satan had God's permission to test Job, Satan went forth and schemed the most severe strategy in his power. He employed two nations (the Sabeans and the Chaldeans), a tornado, and fire from heaven. He arranged to have them striking from all directions at the same time. Job lost 1,000 oxen, 500 donkeys, 7,000 sheep, 3,000 camels, a very great household of servants, seven sons and three daughters, all in one day.[2] Satan meant to make sure that Job would curse God to His face.

Then Job arose, and rent his mantle, and shaved his head, and fell down upon the ground, and worshipped, and said, Naked came I out of my mother's womb, and naked shall I return thither: the L<small>ORD</small> *gave,*

and the LORD hath taken away; blessed be the name of
the LORD. In all this Job sinned not, nor charged God
foolishly (Job 1:20-22).

Job, blissfully unaware that he was being used in a
contest against Satan, could not understand the reason for his suffering. His ignorance of that fact gave
additional validity to the contest. Nevertheless, he
remained faithful, glorifying God and thereby embarrassing Satan. However, Satan again presented himself to the Lord, and requested permission to intensify
the trials.

And the LORD said unto Satan, Hast thou consid-
ered my servant Job, that . . . still he holdeth fast his
integrity, although thou movedst me against him, to
destroy him without cause? And Satan answered
the LORD, and said, Skin for skin, yea, all that a man
hath will he give for his life. But put forth thine hand
now, and touch his bone and his flesh, and he will
curse thee to thy face. And the LORD said unto Satan,
*Behold, he is in thine hand; **but save his life** (Job*
2:3-6).

Again Satan applied the most severe cruelty God
permitted him to use. This time his limit was that he
dared not take Job's life. Job had already lost all his
possessions, most of his servants, and ten children.
All he had left was his wife. Satan even used her as
his mouthpiece, begging Job to *"curse God and die"*
(Job 2:9b). Was there any way for Satan to make things
still more miserable for Job? Yes, there was, and Satan

resorted to it by every possible means.

Job was known far and wide. Three of his friends from different directions *"had made an appointment together to come to mourn with him and to comfort him"* (Job 2:11b). But when they saw his pitiful condition, they were too shocked to speak.

> So they sat down with him upon the ground seven days and seven nights, and none spake a word unto him: for they saw that his grief was very great (Job 2:13).

But Satan's malice knew no mercy! His next strategy was to convince Job's comforters that God was punishing Job for secret, hidden sins. Either Satan himself or one of his evil cohorts disguised himself and came upon their chief spokesman, Eliphaz, at night with truth misapplied. I'll let Eliphaz tell you what he saw and heard.

> Now a thing was secretly brought to me, and mine ear received a little thereof. In thoughts from the visions of the night, when deep sleep falleth on men, Fear came upon me, and trembling, which made all my bones to shake. Then a spirit passed before my face; the hair of my flesh stood up: It stood still, but I could not discern the [disguised] form thereof: an image was before mine eyes, there was silence, and I heard a voice, saying, Shall mortal man be more just than God? shall a man be more pure than his maker? Behold, he put no trust in his servants; and his angels he charged with folly: How much less in them that

dwell in houses of clay, whose foundation is in the dust, which are crushed before the moth? They are destroyed from morning to evening: they perish for ever without any regarding it. Doth not their excellency which is in them go away? they die, even without wisdom (Job 4:12-21).

Satan caused Eliphaz to interpret this as a message from God revealing to him some hidden guilt of Job. It is understandable why he *"could not discern the form"* of the spirit. It was an evil spirit cautiously disguised to hide its identity. Satan managed to persuade all three men to unanimously accuse Job. If Satan had not blocked communications, surely one of the three could have spoken some words of comfort during those seven days.

After a whole week of silence, Job could contain his grief no longer. He cursed the day of his birth, but to curse God found no place in Job's heart. He expressed his yearning to die, but never hinted of suicide. Life to Job was sacred because God is the Author of life.

Then followed three cycles of dialogue. His three friends, now turned into miserable comforters, tried to convince Job that there must be great sin in his life. Job never claimed to be sinless, or self-righteous, but steadfastly confirmed his innocence. His plea was, *"Cause me to understand wherein I have erred." "I have sinned; . . . and why dost thou not pardon my transgression, and take away mine iniquity?"* To his accusers he finally said, *"How long will ye vex my soul, and break me in pieces with words?"* (Job 19:2).

Job spoke of God's omnipotence[3] and omniscience[4] and testified of his own faith and assurance as well.

> *Though he slay me, yet will I trust in him, . . . He also shall be my salvation: . . . (Job 13:15, 16). For I know that my redeemer liveth, and that he shall stand at the latter day upon the earth: and though after my skin worms destroy this body, yet in my flesh* [Luther's German says, *"without my flesh"*] *shall I see God: Whom I shall see for myself, and mine eyes shall behold, and not another; though my reins be consumed within me"* (Job 19:25-27). *But he knoweth the way that I take: when he hath tried me, I shall come forth as gold (Job 23:10).*

Then, in Job 32:6 a young man, Elihu, comes on the scene. He seemed very confident that he was sent by God to set Job and his three friends straight. His speech covers six chapters, 159 verses. He spoke highly of God. Most of his statements about mankind were true enough in themselves, but were grossly misapplied when said of Job. For example: *"What man is like Job, who drinketh up scorning like water? Which goeth in company with the workers of iniquity, and walketh with wicked men"* (Job 34:7, 8). That could **not** be said of Job. Elihu was repetitious, repeating many things the others had already said. He distorted the words of Job to mean things Job never said nor intended.[5]

The very first line following Elihu's last recorded statement, says, *"Then the LORD answered Job out of the whirlwind, and said, Who is this that darkeneth counsel by words without knowledge?"* (Job 38:1, 2). Although God was *answering* Job, He may have been referring to Elihu's monologue, which had *darkened* the six chapters preceding God's question.

Job did repent of some things he had said unadvisedly in response to the relentless pressure of his *"miserable comforters."* However, he had maintained high respect for God, and God later spoke approvingly of Job's words (Job 42:7b). The main thing God did for Job was to redirect his focus from the misery of mortal man to the power and glory of the Creator and His creation.

II. God, the Source of Scientific Proof

The scientific section (Job 38–41) is a significant highlight of this Book. There are no arguments about the guilt or virtue of man. No questions about human suffering are asked or answered. In question format there is revelation about morning stars and angels, the foundations and cornerstone of the earth, the binding and loosing of the sea, and the waters above the earth with their swaddling band of thick darkness. *"Canst thou bind the sweet influences of Pleiades, or loose the bands of Orion? Canst thou bring forth Mazzaroth in his season? or canst thou guide Arcturus with his sons?"* Can you control lightnings or stay the bottles of heaven?[6] The point is, no one but God could do any of these, and no one but God could answer all the questions!

Then He turned to the animals[7] for which God Himself provides food and care: the lion, the raven, the wild goats, the wild ass, the unicorn, the ostrich, the horse, the hawk and the eagle. The implication is that God, who attends to and provides for all of these, certainly cares for and provides all the more for man as well. He had not deserted Job, but had been watching over him with utmost care. In due time He revealed to Job what the contest was all about, and richly rewarded him for his faithfulness during the trial.

> *Moreover the* LORD *answered Job, and said, Shall he that contendeth with the Almighty instruct him? he that reproveth God, let him answer it. Then Job answered the* LORD, *and said, Behold, I am vile; what shall I answer thee? I will lay mine hand upon my mouth. Once have I spoken; but I will not answer: yea, twice; but I will proceed no further (Job 40: 1-5).*

Furthermore, God spoke at length of behemoth and leviathan,[8] monsters of the earth and sea, respectively, whom none but God could control. God cleared Job of all the false accusations the four misinformed men had heaped upon him without mercy, and doubly restored his losses. Satan and his cohorts were silenced by their defeat, and heaven resounded with praises from all the holy angels who had watched the contest with intense interest.

> *So the* Lord *blessed the latter end of Job more than his beginning: . . . He had also seven sons and three daughters. . . . After this lived Job an hundred and forty years, and saw his sons, and his sons' sons, even four generations (Job 42:12, 13, 16).*

What a remarkable record! *"Behold, we count them happy which endure. Ye have heard of the patience of Job, and* **have seen the end of the Lord; that the Lord is very pitiful, and of tender mercy"** (James 5:11). God knew that Job can be trusted for this contest. By it, Job became a living demonstration of God's grace and power, even in the midst of great loss and intense physical suffering.

Questions for Consideration and Discussion

1. Does Satan still accuse faithful saints before God?
2. What qualified Job for such an unusual contest?
3. What motivated Job's wife in her response?
4. Find expressions of faith in Job's statements.
5. Find outstanding doctrinal statements.
6. What kind of spirit appeared to Eliphaz at night?
7. What scientific truths did God reveal by His questions?
8. What did Job confess about his own words?
9. Against whom was God's wrath kindled in the end?

10. Whom did He accept, compliment, and bless? Why?

---

1. Job 1:1	5. Job 33:8, 9; 34:5, 6; 35:2, 3
2. Job 1:13-19	6. Job 38:1-38
3. Job 9:8-12; 26:7-14	7. Job 38:39–39:29
4. Job 28:10-28	8. Job 40:15–41:34

4

One Known as the Friend of God

Abraham believed God, and it was imputed
to him for righteousness: and he was
called the Friend of God
(James 2:23)

Abraham, reckoned in a spiritual sense to be *"the father of us all"* (Romans 4:16b), was chosen to symbolize our heavenly Father offering His only Son for us. Preparation for such a lofty role called for intense testing, through which his faithful wife stood by him all her life. She was first of all his half-sister, being the daughter of his father, but not of his mother; and she became his wife (Genesis 20:12).

Their names for a major part of their lives were Abram and Sarai. They had worshipped idols along with their father Terah (Joshua 24:2) in Ur of the Chaldees. After obeying God's call to leave his homeland and his family, Abram received the promise of becoming a great nation, which required offspring.[1] Sarai, however, was barren from her youth, and

40

would soon be past childbearing age. In spite of many frustrations, and since disappointments are divided and joys are multiplied by sharing them together, they simply consoled each other and waited on the Lord. We have record of at least ten major tests Abram experienced in preparation for his major role. Let us look at those in chronological order.[2]

1. Fourfold Test of Obedience (Genesis 12:1). *"Now the* LORD *had said unto Abram, [1] Get thee out of thy country, [2] and from thy kindred, [3] and from thy father's house, [4] unto a land that I will show thee."* Terah, however, seems to have taken the lead, taking Lot along, and they came to Haran *"and dwelt there"* (Genesis 11:31).

They lived in Haran until Terah died. Then Abram took Sarai his wife, and Lot his brother's son, and all their possessions and came into the land of Canaan.[3] So it took possibly five years to complete the third phase of this test. Abram was 75 and Sarai 65 when they departed out of Haran.

In Canaan, God appeared unto him again with the promise that *"unto thy seed will I give this land."* There Abram built his first altar (Genesis 12:7). But he was not yet separated from Lot, his brother's son, nor was he quite ready to settle down and stay in Canaan. Instead he *"journeyed, going on still toward the south"* (Genesis 12:9). Unfortunately he was moving in the direction of Egypt, which often typifies the world. Beware! Danger ahead!

2. Twofold Test of Trust (Genesis 12:10-20). *"There was a famine in the land: and Abram went* down *into Egypt"* (Genesis 12:10). Now Sarai, even at 65, was still *dangerously* attractive. Abram feared that if they admitted that she was his wife the Egyptians might kill him so Pharaoh could add Sarai to his harem. He therefore told her to pose as his sister. Sure enough, when the Egyptian princes saw her, they commended her to Pharaoh, and she *"was taken into Pharaoh's house"* (Genesis 12:11-20).

Had they fully trusted God to preserve them in Canaan, they would not have gone to Egypt. See Genesis 26:1-3. Second, had they explained that Sarai was his wife, God would surely have protected them both. I am afraid they failed both phases of this test. Even Pharaoh made a better grade upon learning that Sarai was Abram's wife. It was time for Abram to go **back to Bethel!**

3. Test of Values (Genesis 13:8-12). With their departure from Egypt we read for the first time that *"Abram was very rich in cattle, in silver, and in gold"* (Genesis 13:2). For the first time we read that *"Lot also . . . had flocks, and herds, and tents"* (Genesis 13:5), a plurality of everything. Egypt was noted for gain, but not for godliness. Together they now had more cattle than the area between Bethel and Hai could bear. Their herdsmen quarreled for pasture. To avoid strife they had to separate.

God had promised the land to Abram and his

descendants, with no reservations for Lot. But Abram valued relationship more than choice real estate. Therefore he told Lot, "The land is open. You take your choice. I'll take what's left." Lot chose the well-watered plain of Jordan, described *"even as the garden of the Lord, like the land of Egypt"* (Genesis 13:10). He still had Egypt in his heart.

Their separation finally completed test number one, with some demerits for late completion. While he failed the *Twofold Test of Trust,* he made high honors on *the Test of Values.* He's ready now for test number four.

4. Test of Courage (Genesis 14:13-24). Four kings had made war against five kings, and swept through the land racking up victories as they went. Abram got word that Sodom and Gomorrah had been captured, including Lot and his family with all their goods. *"He armed his trained servants, born in his own house, three hundred and eighteen, and pursued them unto Dan. . . . And he brought back all the goods, and also brought again his brother Lot, and his goods, and the women also, and the people"* (Genesis 14:14, 16). That took immeasurable trust and courage. Give him a double A— one for trust and one for courage.

5. Test of Loyalty (Genesis 14:17-24). Melchizedek, king of Salem, who was also the priest of the Most High God, brought bread and wine, and blessed Abram in the name of the Most High God. Abram reverently accepted the refreshments and the blessing, and gave to Melchizedek *"the tenth of the spoils."*[4] But to the king of Sodom, Abram declared with a vow,

> *I have lift up mine hand unto the* LORD, *the most high God, the possessor of heaven and earth, That I will not take from a thread even to a shoelatchet, and that I will not take any thing that is thine, lest thou shouldest say, I have made Abram rich (Genesis 14:22b, 23).*

He recognized that the phenomenal victory was from God and not from man. He used every precaution to give God all the credit. He earned an A on the *Test of Loyalty.*

6. Test of Assurance (Genesis 15:1-6). It may well be that Abram needed some assurance of protection against retaliation from the kings he had defeated by his surprise attack. At least the Lord said, *"Fear not, Abram: I am thy shield, and thy exceeding great reward"* (Genesis 15:1). But there was a greater concern on Abram's heart—and of long standing.

> *And Abram said, Lord* GOD *[Adonia Jehovah], what wilt thou give me, seeing I go childless, and the steward of my house is this Eliezer of Damascus? And Abram said, Behold, to me thou hast given no seed: and, lo, one born in my house is mine heir (Genesis 15:2-3).*

Notice that he addressed God as Adonai Jehovah. *Adonai,* acknowledging God absolutely as his sovereign Master; and *Jehovah,* emphasizing His holiness and all His moral attributes. He combined the most humble, entreatingly reverent title he knew. Then pleadingly, like a tender three-year-old asking Papa for the deepest longing a child could wish for: "I'm yearning for the son You promised me." You see, Sarai was still barren, and by this time she was well past childbearing age. Abram was in his mid-eighties, and time was running out. They had the promise but no child. It looked extremely hopeless. He longed to be reassured of an heir.

God showed him the skies, challenged him to count the stars, and said, *"So shall thy seed be."* At that moment **Abram believed**, and God gave him a passing grade, counting his faith *"for righteousness"* (Genesis 15:6). For his diploma the Lord gave an elaborate confirmation ritual (Genesis 15:9-21), the details of which we must forego. The next test caught both of them by surprise. Great saints often discover that they are after all *ordinary people*, subject to failure.

7. Test of Patience (Genesis 16:1-15). Thus far they may not have been told that Abram's promised son would need to be the son of Sarai as well. She wanted by all means to help Abram obtain his promised son. They lived among a culture where polygamy and concubinage were common practices. And substituting a servant maid seemed even less objectionable. So she offered Hagar as a possible source to obtain a son. It worked. Hagar bore Ishmael. But God had greater plans.

This saintly couple had waited patiently for decades, but failed this particular *Test of Patience.* Ishmael was born when Abram was eighty-six years old. God silently withdrew for thirteen more years. By then Abram had become quite attached to Ishmael (as yet his only son).

8. Threefold Test of Submission (Genesis 17:1-27; 21:12-14). When Abram was ninety-nine years old God appeared to him again, and said, *"I am the Almighty God; walk before me, and be thou perfect."* He changed their names to Abraham and Sarah. He again renewed and expanded His unconditional and everlasting covenant with Abraham and his seed. Nine times in Genesis 17 alone, God refers to it as *"my covenant."* God alone was the Author thereof. In Genesis 17:10-14 He instituted circumcision as the *token* of that special covenant.

When God told him that now He would give him the promised son through Sarah, Abraham feared for his son Ishmael, and said, *"O that Ishmael might live before thee."*

> *And God said, Sarah thy wife shall bear thee a son indeed; and thou shalt call his name Isaac: and I will establish my covenant with him for an **everlasting covenant**, and with his seed after him. And as for Ishmael, I have heard thee: Behold, I have blessed him, and will make him fruitful, and will multiply him exceedingly; twelve princes shall he beget, and I will make him a great nation. But my covenant will I establish with Isaac, which Sarah shall bear unto thee at this set time in the next year (Genesis 17:19-21).*

Notice, God designed that Ishmael should have twelve sons (same as Jacob), while Isaac had only two. *"But my covenant,"* God said, *"will I establish with Isaac, which Sarah shall bear unto thee at this set time in the next year."* Now for the first time Abraham was given an approximate date for the promised son.

Not only did he submit to the idea of having the covenant established in Isaac, but he also accepted circumcision, the newly instituted token of that covenant. Although ninety-nine years old, Abraham immediately went to work and organized a program whereby every male of his entire household, including himself, was circumcised on that self-same day. According to Genesis 14:14, that must have involved several hundred men. We can't imagine what an ordeal that must have been! He has now submitted to two phases of this *Test of Submission..*

Within a year Isaac was born. Some years later, at a feast for the weaning of Isaac, Sarah saw Ishmael mocking Isaac and requested that Abraham cast Hagar and Ishmael out because Ishmael was not to be heir with her son. And the thing was very grievous to Abraham because of Ishmael. He had honored Sarai's suggestion to take Hagar. This time, however, God confirmed her intuitive request, saying,

> *Let it not be grievous in thy sight because of the lad, and because of thy bondwoman; in all that Sarah hath said unto thee, hearken unto her voice; for in Isaac shall thy seed be called (Genesis 21:12).*

So Abraham did as God instructed him, and cast out both Ishmael and Hagar (involving typology beyond the purpose of this writing). Although reluctant, he did pass the final phase of this threefold test.

9. Test of Importunity (Genesis 18:23-32). When God was about to destroy Sodom and Gomorrah, He told Abraham of His intentions. Abraham drew near and (with Lot in mind) began to intercede for the righteous who may have been there. *"That be far from thee . . . , to slay the righteous with the wicked,"* he pled. God promised to spare the city if He found fifty righteous people in Sodom.

"Suppose there are only forty-five, will you then destroy all the city?"

"No," said God, *"if I find forty-five I will not destroy the city."*

Abraham continued pleading, dropping back to forty, then to thirty, then to twenty, and finally to ten.

God said, *"I will not destroy it for ten's sake."*

With that, Abraham was satisfied, and the LORD went His way. God found fewer than ten righteous people in Sodom, and the city was destroyed. But Abraham had persevered long enough and earnestly enough to pass the *Test of Importunity*. He was now prepared for the most crucial test of all.

10. Test of Unshakable Faith (Genesis 22:1-19).

And [God] said, Take now thy son, thine only son Isaac, whom thou lovest, and get thee into the land of Moriah; and offer him there for a burnt offering upon

One Known as the Friend of God 49

one of the mountains which I will tell thee of" (Genesis 22:2).

Notice the three descriptive identifications, each in succession intensifying the severity and pathos of the test. It was *his son*, and since Ishmael was cast out it was his *only son*, it was that miraculous *son of promise* for whom he had waited for decades—the *one* in whom Abraham's seed was to be called. Now, with Ishmael gone, Abraham's *fatherly love* and hope for the future were totally wrapped up in Isaac. Yet God said, "Offer him for a burnt offering." What a test of faith!

With no recorded evidence of any hesitation, *"Abraham rose up early in the morning . . . and went unto the place of which God had told him."*

> Abraham built an altar there, and laid the wood in order, and bound Isaac his son, and laid him on the altar upon the wood. And Abraham stretched forth his hand, and took the knife to slay his son. And the angel of the LORD called unto him out of heaven, and said, Abraham, Abraham: and he said, Here am I. And he said, Lay not thine hand upon the lad, neither do thou any thing unto him: for now I know that thou fearest God, seeing thou hast not withheld thy son, thine only son from me (Genesis 22:9b-12).

This was a tremendous act of faith, *"accounting that God was able to raise him up, even from the dead; from whence also he received him in a figure"* (Hebrews 11:19). This is probably the only time God ever asked anyone to offer a human sacrifice. This was **not** an offering for sin, but a consecration offering, by which Abraham proved his loyalty and total obedience to God. It may have been the most significant role Abraham ever played, and the hardest test he ever had, but he passed it with a perfect score.

God seems to have chosen Abraham, the spiritual *"father of us all"* (Romans 4:16), to illustrate (and experience) what God planned to do for lost humanity. Before the Holy Tri-unity created the world,[5] they had already planned that He who was **equal with God**[6] would temporarily lay down His equality and, by incarnation, become the Father's Son.[7] Then He would take *"upon him the form of a servant, . . . made in the likeness of men"* (Philippians 2:7), for the express purpose of becoming the crucified Sacrifice for the sins of men.

That sacred plan seemed to be illustrated in Abraham's experience, so that even Old Testament saints could understand and believe the coming of our Savior and Redeemer.

> *For God so loved the world, that he gave his only begotten Son, that whosoever believeth in him should not perish, but have everlasting life (John 3:16).*

> *Neither is there salvation in any other: for there is none other name under heaven given among men, whereby we must be saved (Acts 4:12).*

Questions for Consideration and Discussion

1. Why was Abram to leave his country and kindred?
2. Why did God speak of Isaac as "thine only son" (Genesis 22:1)?
3. What problems did Abram inherit from having been in Egypt?
4. Did Abram owe Lot the courtesy of first choice of the land?
5. For what reason, greater than pasture, was separation required?
6. What consequences did Lot suffer from his choice?
7. What was the significance of the *covenantal sign* given to Abram?
8. What was the significance of Abram giving tithes to Melchizedek?
9. What was the deepest yearning in Abram's heart at that time?
10. Why did God so long delay giving the promised son?

---

1. Genesis 12:2
2. I give credit to Brother Willard Mayer who brought these ten tests to my attention in 1953. I cannot reproduce them accurately, but have tried to follow the general trend, with a few alterations and additions.
3. Genesis 12:5
4. Genesis 14:18-20; Hebrews 7:4
5. Hebrews 1:2; John 1:3, 10; 1 Corinthians 8:6; Ephesians 2:10; 3:9
6. Philippians 2:6
7. Psalm 2:7

A Classic Couple With Partiality Problems

Isaac loved Esau . . . Rebekah loved Jacob
(Genesis 25:28)

Characteristics of Rebekah

I always marvel at Rebekah's first recorded activities. Abraham had told his faithful servant to take a wife for Isaac from Abraham's kindred. When he arrived at the well in Haran, he prayed a very unusual prayer. Who would expect a lady, when asked by a total stranger for a drink from her pitcher, to immediately volunteer to draw water for ten thirsty camels? That is what this servant asked for, as a sign that this is the one whom God had appointed to be Isaac's wife. While he was yet praying, Rebekah came, went down to the well, filled her pitcher and came up.

*And the servant ran to meet her, and said, Let me, I pray thee, drink a little water of thy pitcher. And she said, Drink, my lord: and **she hasted**, and let down her pitcher upon her hand, and gave him drink. And when she had done giving him drink, she said, I* *will draw* water *for thy camels also, until they have done drinking. And* **she hasted,** *and emptied her pitcher into the trough, and* **ran again** *unto the well to draw* water, *and drew for* **all his camels** *(Genesis 24:17-20).*

What an industrious demonstration, with no thought of earning herself a husband!

And the man wondering at her held his peace, to wit whether the LORD *had made his journey prosperous or not (Genesis 24:21).*

Imagine how many trips she must have made between the well and the trough, as the servant and his men watched in wonder. While rushing back and forth, she may have wondered what ever possessed her to make such a commitment. The servant did not yet know who she was, but when the camels were done drinking, he inquired. Sure enough, she was a granddaughter of Abraham's brother, the very family from whom he was to seek a wife for Isaac. This was not a coincidence; it was a direct answer from God. *"And the damsel ran, and told them of her mother's house these things"* (Genesis 24:28).

After a family conference, Rebekah, with her nurse inherited from home, went with the servant and his men (an estimated five hundred miles) to Canaan.

Characteristics of Isaac[1]

It was evening, and Isaac, a godly man of prayer, was out in the field meditating. When he looked up, *"behold, the camels were coming."* Rebekah also looked up and saw Isaac coming. The servant told her, *"It is my master."* She immediately dismounted from her camel, took a veil and covered herself, to reverently meet her husband-to-be in proper decorum.

The romance was very brief. The Bible says that Isaac took Rebekah, and she became his wife; **and he loved her.** He never took a concubine, nor a second wife. In his undivided love and loyalty to Rebekah he was a shining example.

Faithful But Not Faultless

During a famine, Isaac started toward Egypt as Abraham had done. He came to Gerar at the southern end of the promised land, where the LORD graciously stopped him, saying,

> Go not down into Egypt; dwell in the land which I shall tell thee of: sojourn in this land, and I will be with thee, and will bless thee; for unto thee, and unto thy seed, I will give all these countries, and I will perform the oath which I sware unto Abraham thy father; and I will make thy seed to multiply as the stars of heaven, and will give unto thy seed all these countries; and in thy seed shall all the nations of the earth be blessed (Genesis 26:2b-4).

While Isaac dwelt at Gerar, he made the same mistake Abraham had made twice,[2] saying that his wife was his sister (Genesis 26:7). Both were reproved, each by the Abimelech of their respective days. Isaac sowed and prospered there, and became so great that Abimelech said, *"Go from us; for thou art much mightier than we."* Isaac was especially noted for digging wells, having dug again the wells that Abraham's servants had made, which the Philistines had filled with earth, and he also dug four new wells.

> *And Isaac's servants digged in the valley, and found there a well of springing water [an artesian]. And the herdmen of Gerar did strive with Isaac's herdmen, saying, The water is ours: and he called the name of the well Esek; because they strove with him. And they digged another well, and strove for that also: and he called the name of it Sitnah. And he removed from thence, and digged another well; and for that they strove not: and he called the name of it Rehoboth; and he said, For now the LORD hath made room for us, and we shall be fruitful in the land (Genesis 26:19-22).*

There is no mention of an altar at Gerar, but Isaac maintained a godly, nonresistant life. Now notice what happened as soon as he came back into the heart of the land where God wanted him.

> *And he went up from thence to Beersheba. And the LORD appeared unto him **the same night,** and said, I am the God of Abraham thy father: fear not, for I am with thee, and will bless thee, and multiply thy seed for my servant Abraham's sake. And he builded an altar there, and called upon the name of the LORD, and pitched his tent there: and there Isaac's*

servants digged a well (Genesis 26:23-25).

Notice the order of mention: first the altar, putting God first and calling upon the name of the LORD before pitching his tent. Abimelech came all the way to Beersheba to make peace, and give special recognition to Isaac, because he saw that the LORD was with him. That same day Isaac's servants came, from digging another well, and told him, *"We have found water"* (Genesis 26:32). Isaac was a man of many wells, but only Christ provides *"rivers of living water"* (John 7:38).

Rebekah had been barren the first 20 years of their married life. But Isaac, trusting in God, entreated the LORD for Rebekah, and the LORD answered with twins. They were opposites in many ways, and God had decreed that *"the elder shall serve the younger"* (Genesis 25:23).

Partiality Problems

Being blessed with children should strengthen the bonds of a marriage, but the contrast in these twins erupted into a conflict.

*And the boys grew: and Esau was a cunning hunter, a man of the field; and Jacob was a plain man, dwelling in tents. And **Isaac loved Esau**, because he did eat of his venison: but **Rebekah loved Jacob** (Genesis 25:27, 28).*

The Bible says nothing about Rebekah's love for Isaac. It does tell us that Isaac loved Rebekah (Genesis 24:67), and that Rebekah loved Jacob. It was right for her to love her son, but not at the expense of loyalty and respect for her husband. Neither was Isaac without fault in the matter.

When Isaac was old and nearly blind, he wanted to *make his will,* and prepare to die. Saintly as he was, he was still human. Had he forgotten God's message to Rebekah, that their elder son was to serve the younger; and that Esau had already sold his birthright to Jacob?[3] Was Esau's venison more impressive than God's design? Isaac asked Esau to prepare him venison such as he loved, *"that my soul may bless **thee** before I die"* (Genesis 27:1-4)

Rebekah, overhearing those instructions, hastened to intervene in behalf of her favorite son. Instead of speaking to Isaac, she plotted with Jacob to outwit their honorable husband and father.[4] Jacob obtained the blessing, but not in the way that God intended to give it to him. It led to a family disaster for which they all paid dearly.

When Isaac realized what had happened, he *"trembled very exceedingly,"* evidently sensing his own error. Immediately, he confirmed that the patriarchal blessing should remain upon Jacob (Genesis 27:33). Esau resolved that when Isaac died, he was going to kill Jacob (Genesis 27:41). When Rebekah heard that, she immediately made plans to send Jacob to Haran for a wife. Isaac agreed, and passed on to Jacob the unconditional Abrahamic covenant and blessing (Genesis 28:1-5) before sending him. Jacob's departure was the last that Rebekah saw of him.

The Bible is silent about the remaining years of their lives. Only Isaac's death, and burial (Genesis 35:28-29) are recorded after Jacob's departure. Of Rebekah we find even less: only the historic place of her burial (Genesis 49:31). Isaac died at the age of one hundred eighty, at about the time Joseph was delivered from prison in Egypt.[5] In age, he surpassed Abraham and Jacob. Of the three, only Isaac never crossed the borders of Canaan, and only Isaac never engaged in polygamy or concubinage. God wrought wonders through Isaac and Rebekah in spite of their human failures.

May Isaac's love for Rebekah and his loyalty to her remind us that Christ's love for His church is absolutely true and pure, whereas our love for Christ is often faulty or delinquent. Sometimes we may be as fervent as Rebekah was when she watered the camels, and at other times as deceptive as she was in disguising Jacob to obtain the patriarchal blessing.

Questions for Consideration or Discussion
1. What problems were caused by the partiality?
2. How old was Isaac when he married Rebekah?
3. How old was he when the twins were born?
4. What kept him from crossing the borders of Canaan?
5. What did God tell him about going down into Egypt?
6. What did Isaac do when the Philistines stole his wells?

7. What testimony did he leave with the people at Gerar?

8. Who appeared to him his first night back at Beersheba?

9. In what three aspects did he surpass Abraham and Jacob?

10. Why is there silence about the latter years of Isaac and Rebekah?

---

1. Isaac had been mentioned in Chapter Four, and more widely discussed in my earlier volume, *Seeing Christ in the Old Testament*.

2. Genesis 12:13; 20:2

3. Genesis 25:29-34

4. Genesis 27:6-29

5. Jacob, sixty years younger than Isaac (Genesis 25:26), was 120 when Isaac died. Ten years later he was 130, when he stood before Pharaoh in Egypt (47:9), and Joseph had reigned about ten years (cf. 41:29-30; 45:6).

6

The Twin With Two Names and Two Natures

*Is not he rightly named **Jacob**?*
for he hath supplanted me these two times:
he took away my birthright; and, behold,
now he hath taken away my blessing . . .
(Genesis 27:36b).

*Thy name shall be called no more **Jacob**, but **Israel**: for*
as a prince hast thou power with God and
with men, and hast prevailed
(Genesis 32:28b).

Jacob usually had his way, whether by decree or deceit, faith or fraud. He was the second-born son of Isaac, struggled prenatally with his twin brother, and was born with his hand gripping his brother's heel. Therefore he was named Jacob [supplanter] (Genesis 25:26).

"*Esau* [his twin brother] *was a cunning hunter, a man of the field,*" but Jacob, Rebekah's favorite son, was content at home. One day Jacob had prepared a savory stew when Esau came home from the field, faint and hungry.

"Ah, give me a bowl of that red stew," exclaimed Esau.

"Sell me your birthright," bargained Jacob.

"Birthright," scoffed Esau, "What good can a birthright be to me? I'm starved!"

"Swear to me this day," Jacob continued.

Esau sware unto him, selling his birthright to Jacob. Thus Esau despised his birthright, and Jacob gained a bargain. With a kinder heart he could have given the stew as a brotherly gesture and won a friend. But Jacob was inclined toward *bargains*, not brothers. All it took was a cleverly designed offer when Esau was in a reckless mood. Esau readily sealed the deal with an oath and went his merry way. God also had a hand in this peaceable transaction in keeping with His prediction that *"the elder* [twin] *shall serve the younger"* (Genesis 25:23b).

Jacob, as a man with two natures, typifies born-again Christians, who also have two natures. Christians must learn to bring their self-will under God's control, and that is what God was trying to teach Jacob. His self-centered characteristics frequently took the lead. But in his second nature he was deeply spiritual and truly worshipped God, as we shall see.

In Isaac's life story we saw how Jacob had obtained his father's blessing by deceit. That very act cost Jacob at least twenty (some think forty) years of exile from the Promised Land. Meanwhile Esau nursed his consuming hatred for at least twenty years before he and Jacob were finally reconciled. Surely God had a better way for both of them (and for their mother), if only they would have trusted Him completely.

Jacob Flees From Esau

Hearing of Esau's threat,[1] Jacob fled for his life to Uncle Laban, at Haran. Driven by fear, he possibly reached Bethel the first night, a distance of fifty miles or more. He must have been exhausted, sad, and lonely. Stones were his pillow and the open sky his canopy. There God communicated with him in a dream, showing him a ladder that connected heaven and earth, with the angels of God ascending and descending upon it.

> *And, behold, the* LORD *stood above it, and said, I am the* LORD *God of Abraham thy father, and the God of Isaac: the land whereon thou liest, to thee will I give it, and to thy seed; and thy seed shall be as the dust of the earth, and thou shalt spread abroad to the west, and to the east, and to the north, and to the south: and in thee and in thy seed shall all the families of the earth be blessed. And, behold, I am with thee, and will keep thee in all places whither thou goest, and will bring thee again into this land; for I will not leave thee, until I have done that which I have spoken to thee of (Genesis 28:13-15).*

Jacob awoke, gripped with awe and grateful reverence. The stone on which he had rested his head he anointed with oil, setting it up for a pillar and naming the place Beth-el (House of God). In response to God's marvelous promise, Jacob made a vow, committing himself with confidence into God's care, saying, *"and of all that thou shalt give me I will surely give the tenth unto thee."* Comforted, and assured of God's protecting care, he went on his way toward Haran, more than four hundred lonely miles farther. The whole journey was quite an undertaking for a man more adapted to the tent than to the field.

No wonder he lifted up his voice, and wept with joy, when he met *Cousin Rachel* with *Uncle Laban's* sheep (Genesis 29:1-12). *"And Laban said to him, Surely thou art my bone and my flesh. And he abode with him the space of a month"* (Genesis 29:14), perhaps helping as a herdsman.

When Laban asked what wages he desired, Jacob said, *"I will serve thee seven years for Rachel thy younger daughter."* Jacob was not always grasping for bargains at minimum cost. He was also generous and serious; willing to work and to wait. Not many men his age would volunteer to work and wait seven years for the wife they really wanted!

Deception Breeds Deception

And Jacob served seven years for Rachel; and they seemed unto him but a few days, for the love he had to her (Genesis 29:20).

Things seemed to be working out as Jacob had

planned. However, the law of sowing and reaping was still in effect. God's blessings upon Jacob at Bethel did not justify his role in deceiving his father. His reaping was about to begin. After serving Laban seven years, for Rachel whom he dearly loved, Jacob asked for a fulfillment of their agreement. We are told that weddings called for a festival of seven days. At the end of the first day Laban presented the bride to the groom, completely veiled.

> *And it came to pass, that in the morning, behold, it was Leah: and he said to Laban, What is this thou hast done unto me? did not I serve with thee for Rachel? wherefore then hast thou beguiled me? And Laban said, It must not be so done in our country, to give the younger before the **firstborn**. Fulfil her week, and we will give thee this also for the service which thou shalt serve with me yet seven other years (Genesis 29:25-27).*

Laban was not as pliable as Isaac had been. If there was such a custom at Haran, Laban should have explained that to Jacob before accepting his offer. This was an injustice for which there was no excuse. It was worse than what Jacob had done to his blind father, but Jacob was learning that misdeeds do have undesirable consequences.

How did Rachel feel by this time? Didn't she know that Jacob expected to marry her? When and how did Rachel (and even Leah!) discover which daughter Laban was going to give him? These are things we don't know, but we do know that Jacob was deceived—and frustrated!

"Fulfill her week." Let the seven-day festivity continue with no embarrassing interruption. After Leah's celebration is all over, we will quietly and secretly add Rachel to the deal. That sounds cheap! Jacob hardly felt like celebrating, but he endured the adjustment. What else could he do? The seven years had seemed short and pleasant. But these seven days were marred by the pain of deception. God never designed polygamy. **Two** (not three or four) **shall be one!**

Multiple wives make for unwholesome competition. Jacob had been Rebekah's *favorite* son; now he had a *favorite* wife, a *favoritism* that bore undesirable consequences. When the LORD saw that Leah suffered for lack of love, He compensated her with children. With each birth Leah rejoiced with the hope that now Jacob would love her. But Jacob, having committed himself to marry Rachel, had cultivated a love for her that he could not duplicate for anyone else. He was reaping a harvest from the sowing he had done at Beersheba seven years earlier.

His wives both suffered: Leah for lack of love, Rachel for lack of children. She said to Jacob, *"Give me children, or else I die."* The competition was so great that Rachel resorted to giving her handmaid Bilhah to Jacob, and claimed two sons obtained through her. In the meantime Leah had temporarily left bearing. Not satisfied with four sons, she also resorted to her handmaid Zilpah, and claimed two sons through her. Later Leah had two more sons and one daughter.

And God remembered Rachel, and God hearkened to her, and opened her womb. And she conceived, and bare a son; and said, God hath taken away my reproach: And she called his name Joseph; and said, The LORD shall add to me another son (Genesis 30:22-24).

Joseph was the gem of the family. He may have been Jacob's eleventh son, but he was Rachel's firstborn, and so outstanding in character that he inherited the birthright without trying (1 Chronicles 5:1, 2).

I claim no familiarity with, nor confidence in, those *magic schemes* that Jacob practiced in efforts to increase his own flocks (Genesis 30:37-43). I am persuaded that God was exercising His Abrahamic promise upon Jacob,[2] and blessed him *in spite of* his schemes, rather than *in response to* them. Without those schemes God may have blessed Jacob even more, possibly changing the hot displeasure of Laban and his sons into brotherly blessings. God knows what might have been.

Jacob Starts for the Promised Land

And Jacob beheld the countenance of Laban, and, behold, it was not toward him as before. And the LORD said unto Jacob, Return unto the land of thy fathers, and to thy kindred; and I will be with thee.

And Jacob sent and called Rachel and Leah to the field unto his flock, And said unto them, I see your father's countenance, that it is not toward me as before; but the God of my father hath been with me. And ye know that with all my power I have served your father (Genesis 31:2-6).

Notice that God is still at work, calling Jacob back to the Promised Land. Rachel and Leah agreed with Jacob. Together they planned and actually departed for Canaan without telling Laban. The New Bible Commentary says Mount Gilead is more than three hundred miles from Haran. They suggest that Jacob probably had his flocks moving strategically in that direction for several weeks, and that the family remained in their tents to forestall detection of the intended escape. Then at the zero hour they mounted swift camels and caught up with the flocks.

Laban had been away shearing sheep. Three days later he heard of Jacob's departure. It took him another seven days in hot pursuit to overtake them in Mount Gilead. We wonder what would have happened at that meeting if God had not warned Laban the night before to be careful in his conduct toward Jacob (Genesis 31:24). Even so, there were angry words, but no physical combat.

What did Laban want with images that he called his gods (Genesis 31:30)? And why had Rachel taken them? Gods that can be stolen are nothing but dormant trinkets. Not knowing that Rachel had them,

Jacob said, *"With whomsoever thou findest thy gods, let him not live."* In light of that commitment, what would they have done to Rachel if her theft had been discovered? Did Jacob's statement possibly contribute to Rachel's early death[3] a few months later? Be that as it may, we rejoice that Jacob and Laban could part with a covenant of peace (Genesis 31:43-55).

The Reconciliation of Jacob and Esau

"Jacob went on his way, and the angels of God met him" (Genesis 32:1). God knew that another crisis lay just ahead. Esau was coming with four hundred men. "Jacob was greatly afraid and distressed." His two natures sprang into action. His self-sufficient, scheming nature acted first, quickly dividing the people, the flocks, herds, and camels into two bands. He said, *"If Esau come to the one company, and smite it, then the other company which is left shall escape."* After that, with his spiritual nature, he plunged into earnest prayer.

> *And Jacob said, O God of my father Abraham, and God of my father Isaac, the Lord which saidst unto me, Return unto thy country, and to thy kindred, and I will deal well with thee: I am not worthy of the least of all the mercies, and of all the truth, which thou hast showed unto thy servant; for with my staff I passed over this Jordan; and now I am become two bands. Deliver me, I pray thee, from the hand of my brother, from the hand of Esau: for I fear him, lest he will come and smite me, and the mother with the chil-*

dren. And thou saidst, I will surely do thee good, and make thy seed as the sand of the sea, which cannot be numbered for multitude (Genesis 32:9-12).

Jacob's two natures worked simultaneously: the spirit in fervent prayer, the flesh in feverish scheming. He prepared an enormous gift of goats, sheep, camels, cattle, and donkeys: 580 animals. He divided them into five droves, each species in a drove by itself, and told his servants to put a space between drove and drove, for maximum effect upon Esau. Moreover, he instructed each set of servants what to say when Esau asks to whom these herds belong.

*Then thou shalt say, They be thy servant Jacob's; it is a present sent unto my lord Esau: and, behold, also he is behind us. . . . For he said, **I will appease him with the present** that goeth before me, and afterward I will see his face; peradventure he will accept of me (Genesis 32:18, 20).*

Notice, he still said "*I* will appease him." He was still scheming. That night he sent his family and all that he had over the ford Jabbok, and Jacob was left alone. "*There wrestled a man with him until the breaking of the day.*" That Man, called "the angel" in Hosea 12:4, must have been the Lord Jesus Christ Himself. He could say with authority, "*Thy name shall be called no more Jacob, but Israel: for as a prince hast thou power with God and with men, and hast prevailed.*"

Jacob asked for the Man's name. The Man did not

tell His name, but He did bless Jacob. Whereupon Jacob said, *"I have seen God face to face, and my life is preserved"* (Genesis 32:30).

What was God seeking to obtain from Jacob? This was a spiritual contest, not a physical one. The Lord wrestled till daybreak for the control of Jacob's will, his trust, and his confidence. *"And when he saw that he prevailed not against him, he touched the hollow of his thigh; and the hollow of Jacob's thigh* [the strongest member of his body] *was out of joint"* (Genesis 32:25). Flesh must be broken that faith may be strong.

God may have used Jacob's pathetic limp to melt the heart of Esau. Jacob marching like a mighty soldier would have been no threat at all to Esau and his four hundred men. But when Jacob came limping, and bowing seven times with his face to the ground, the spirit of revenge drained out of Esau. The limping and bowing which God supervised was more effective than all Jacob's planning and gifts had been. It was a fulfillment of Isaac's blessing to Esau: *"When thou shalt have the dominion, thou shalt break his [Jacob's] yoke from off thy neck" (Genesis 27:40).*

And Esau ran to meet him, and embraced him, and fell on his neck, and kissed him: and they wept (Genesis 33:4).

Then follows a beautiful story of reconciliation after many years of animosity between the twin sons of Isaac. But Jacob accepted no assistance from Esau. Was it just that he felt unworthy of Esau's offers, or was it still a lack of trust? He promised Esau to come to him in the land of Seir, but instead of that he *"journeyed to Succoth, and built him an house, . . . and he erected there an altar"* (Genesis 33:14, 20). This was Jacob's first recorded altar.

Back to Bethel

Although he was now within the borders of the Promised Land, he was not yet where God wanted him to be. Things did not go well for him. His sons, after making a false peace with the Shechemites, broke their promise and annihilated the village (Genesis 34). In spite of the unconditional covenant already conveyed upon Jacob (Genesis 28:13-15), and the promise of God's protection repeated to him several times, Jacob's faith buckled again. He said, *"I being few in number, they shall gather themselves together against me, and slay me; and I shall be destroyed, I and my house"* (Genesis 34:30). How can frail man put confidence in his own strength, yet tremble in the care of God Almighty?

And God said unto Jacob, Arise, go up to Bethel, and dwell there: and make there an altar unto God, that appeared unto thee when thou fleddest from the face of Esau thy brother. Then Jacob said unto his household, and to all that were with him, Put away the strange gods that are among you, and be clean, and change your garments (Genesis 35:1, 2).

Jacob feared to go up to Bethel with the excess

baggage which he knew does not meet with God's approval. They first disposed of their strange gods, *"and all their ear rings which were in their ears; and Jacob hid them under the oak which was by Shechem"* (Genesis 35:4). Having disposed of their idols and ornaments, they went to Bethel and there he built an altar. We read nothing of an altar all the while they lived at Haran, but this was the second one in the few months since returning to the Promised Land.

> *And God said unto him, I am God Almighty: be fruitful and multiply; a nation and a company of nations shall be of thee, and kings shall come out of thy loins; And the land which I gave Abraham and Isaac, to thee I will give it, and to thy seed after thee will I give the land (Genesis 35:11, 12).*

Perhaps the saddest experience in Jacob's life was when his sons deceived him about the fate of Joseph whom they had sold into Egypt. They dipped his coat of many colors in the blood of a goat and brought it to Jacob, saying, *"This have we found"* (Genesis 37:14-35). Jacob and his mother had cunningly deceived Isaac with the hairy skins of a kid (Genesis 27:15-27). Now his sons mercilessly deceived Jacob with the bloodied coat of his favorite son. Jacob was still reaping!

Their act was much more cruel than what Jacob had done! Deception bears grievous results, and sin pays cruel dividends! For more than twenty years Jacob mourned intensely for Joseph before he learned that Joseph was still alive. And all that while, the ten sons must have endured the torture of their guilt. How calloused can a human heart get? Truly, *"The heart is deceitful above all things, and desperately wicked: who can know it?"* (Jeremiah 17:9).

Jacob lived his last seventeen years in Egypt, where at the age of one hundred forty-seven years he called his sons to his bedside, and conveyed upon each one a prophetic blessing. Then *"he gathered up his feet into the bed, and yielded up the ghost, and was gathered unto his people"* (Genesis 49:33). The Egyptians spent forty days embalming his body, and for seventy days they mourned his death. Then "a very great company" of chariots and horsemen carried the body back to Canaan for burial.

The seven days of professional and "grievous mourning"[4] enroute to the burial seems superficial and unbecoming for people of God. It was obviously intended as an honor to the departed one, but for true believers, physical death is a graduation to life eternal. The sting of death is removed by faith in Christ. Honest tears have a rightful place at any funeral, but a believer's sorrows are tempered with joys that are even deeper and greater than their sorrow. *"Precious in the sight of the LORD is the death of his saints"* (Psalm 116:15). I believe Heaven celebrated the homecoming of Jacob.

Questions for Consideration and Discussion

1. Had Isaac forgotten what God had told Rebekah (Genesis 25:23)?

2. What were Rebekah's options about Isaac blessing Esau?

3. Explain God's blessing at Bethel in light of Jacob's guilt?

4. What was God's attitude toward Jacob's poplar rods (30:37-43)?

5. Why did Rachel steal Laban's gods upon leaving Haran?

6. Why did Laban look for them upon pursuing Jacob?

7. Who was the man who wrestled with Jacob at Peniel?

8. What was the Man seeking to do for Jacob?

9. What happened to Jacob's birthright when he met Esau?

10. What all did Jacob dispose of before going to Bethel?

---

1. Genesis 27:41
2. Genesis 28:4, 5, 13, 14
3. Genesis 35:19
4. Genesis 50:10, 11

The Most Christlike
Son of Israel

*These are the generations of Jacob. **Joseph**, being seventeen years old, was feeding the flock with his brethren; and the lad was with the sons of Bilhah, and with the sons of Zilpah, his father's wives: and Joseph brought unto his father their evil report. Now Israel loved Joseph more than all his children, because he was the son of his old age: and he made him a coat of many colours (Genesis 37:2, 3).*

At the age of seventeen, Joseph heads the list of the generations of Jacob. Genesis 37:2-28 records eight characteristics of Joseph that were similar to those of Jesus. (1) He was feeding his father's flock; (2) he testified of men's evil doings; (3) he was the most beloved son; (4) he was hated by his brothers; (5) he shared prophetic revelations; (6) his brothers envied him; (7) he sought and found his brothers; (8) and he was sold by Judah for money.

His brothers, having sold Joseph, took his colorful coat, probably ripped it to random pieces like the work of a wild beast, dipped it into the blood of a goat, and took it to Jacob. Jacob rent his clothes, put on sackcloth, and mourned for many days. His sons in their hypocritical guilt could not comfort him. For twenty years they kept their bloody secret! Jacob assumed that God's special plan for Joseph had been frustrated. But God remained in control, working His plan throughout Joseph's life.

Purity Overrules Misconduct

And Joseph was brought down to Egypt; and Potiphar, an officer of Pharaoh, captain of the guard, an Egyptian, bought him of the hands of the Ishmeelites, which had brought him down thither. And the LORD was with Joseph, and he was a prosperous man; and he was in the house of his master the Egyptian. And his master saw that the LORD was with him, and that the LORD made all that he did to prosper in his hand. And Joseph found grace in his sight, and he served him: and he made him overseer over his house, and all that he had he put into his hand (Genesis 39:1-4).

Whether son, slave, or steward, Joseph lived above the circumstances of his environment and became master of the situation. First, he became overseer of all that Potiphar had, except his wife. Being the wife of his master, she may have assumed some authority over Joseph. Day by day she tried to seduce him with verbal requests, and finally by physical force, to lie with her. But Joseph steadfastly refused to submit to her demands, or to sin against God. When she laid hold on his garment to force him, he left the garment in her hands, and fled from her pursuit.

In revenge she framed a lie, posing as the victim of an attack by Joseph. The garment she had plucked from his body she presented to her husband as *evidence* of an attack, and he cast Joseph into prison. If Potiphar had genuinely believed her story, probably he would have executed Joseph. Imprisoning him was enough to *save face* for Potiphar's wife.

"But the LORD was with Joseph" in prison, using him as a specimen of righteousness and at the same time preparing him for even greater service. Inseparable from God, he was a useful servant wherever he was. *"And the keeper of the prison committed all the prisoners that were in the prison into Joseph's hand; and whatsoever they did there, he was the doer of it"* (Genesis 39:22).

From Prisoner to Prophet

Two prisoners are singled out as special figures: Pharaoh's butler and baker. They each had a dream foretelling their destiny, which Joseph correctly interpreted for them. The butler (depicting God's mercy for believers) was restored and the baker (illustrating divine justice for unbelievers) was hanged (Genesis 40:1-23), exactly as Joseph predicted.

We have no record of how long Joseph had been in prison before the butler's release, but the butler forgot about Joseph for two full years. Then God gave Pharaoh two dreams that none of his magicians could interpret. Thereupon the butler remembered Joseph and told Pharaoh how Joseph had correctly interpreted both his and the baker's dreams two years earlier.

> *Then Pharaoh sent and called Joseph, and they brought him hastily* **out of the dungeon:** *and he shaved himself, and changed his raiment, and came in unto Pharaoh. And Pharaoh said unto Joseph, I have dreamed a dream, and there is none that can interpret it: and I have heard say of thee, that thou canst understand a dream to interpret it. And Joseph answered Pharaoh, saying, It is not in me: God shall give Pharaoh an answer of peace (Genesis 41:14-16).*

Pharaoh's dreams were extensive and thorough. Both illustrated the same thing, being doubled for emphasis.[1] Both foretold the coming of seven extremely fruitful years, followed by seven years of very grievous famine. Joseph, as God's mouthpiece to man, explained them fully and gave instructions how to cope with the situation.

From Prophet to Prime Minister

Pharaoh immediately made Joseph ruler over all the land of Egypt, changed his name to Zaphnathpaaneah, and gave him the priest's daughter to wife. At that time Joseph was thirty years old, corresponding with the age of Jesus when He began His ministry. [2]

And in the seven plenteous years the earth brought forth by handfuls. And he gathered up all the food of the seven years, which were in the land of Egypt, and laid up the food in the cities: the food of the field, which was round about every city, laid he up in the same. And Joseph gathered corn as the sand of the sea, very much, until he left numbering; for it was without number (Genesis 41:47-49).

And the seven years of dearth began to come, according as Joseph had said: and the dearth was in all lands; but in all the land of Egypt there was bread. And when all the land of Egypt was famished, the people cried to Pharaoh for bread: and Pharaoh said unto all the Egyptians, Go unto Joseph; what he saith to you, do. And the famine was over all the face of the earth: And Joseph opened all the storehouses, and sold unto the Egyptians; and the famine waxed sore in the land of Egypt. And all countries came into Egypt to Joseph for to buy corn; because that the famine was so sore in all lands (Genesis 41:54-57).

Preserved by God to Preserve Others

Canaan was also ravished by the famine. Ten of Joseph's brothers came to buy corn in Egypt. It was approximately twenty years since they had sold Joseph into slavery. The possibility of Joseph being the ruler of Egypt was far from their minds. They came *"and bowed down themselves before him, with their faces to the earth."* Joseph knew them, and remembered the dreams for which his brothers had hated him.

Now Joseph was God's instrument to prove his own brothers.

Joseph spoke to his brothers through an interpreter, saying, "Ye are spies; to see the nakedness of the land ye are come." They explained their family status as twelve sons of one man, of whom the youngest is at home with their father, and one *is no more.* *"That is it . . . , Ye are spies: hereby ye shall be proved: By the life of Pharaoh ye shall not go forth hence, except your youngest brother come hither"* (Genesis 42:14, 15).

"He put them all together into ward three days." Did he have secret means of hearing their conversation during their time *in ward*? Perhaps he sought evidence of repentance for what they had done to him. Nor was he alone in this effort, for God most certainly sought their repentance through him. Joseph was especially interested in knowing how they were treating Benjamin.

> *And Joseph said unto them the third day, This do, and live; for I fear God: If ye be true men, let one of your brethren be bound in the house of your prison: go ye, carry corn for the famine of your houses: But bring your youngest brother unto me; so shall your words be verified, and ye shall not die. And they did so.*

> *And they said one to another, We are verily guilty concerning our brother, in that we saw the anguish of his soul, when he besought us, and we would not hear; therefore is this distress come upon us. And*

Reuben answered them, saying, Spake I not unto you, saying, Do not sin against the child; and ye would not hear? therefore, behold, also his blood is required. And they knew not that Joseph understood them; for he spake unto them by an interpreter (Genesis 42:18-23).

Joseph turned from them and wept. When he returned, he bound Simeon before their eyes, and kept him in prison until the others came again, bringing Benjamin with them. His purpose for selecting Simeon is not revealed to us, but I suspect they who had first-hand knowledge may have at least partially understood.

Joseph commanded his sevants to fill their sacks with corn, restore every man's money into his sack, and give them provision for the way. They loaded their donkeys and departed. When they got home and found that every man's money was restored, they feared greatly. Guilty souls are easily frightened even by beneficence.

They told Jacob all that happened to them in Egypt, how the lord of the land spoke roughly to them and accused them of being spies. They explained how he kept Simeon in prison, and how he demanded that they bring Benjamin. None of them knew the yearning of Joseph's heart, nor ever suspected the half of what he was really planning to do for them. God's mill grinds slowly, but thoroughly.

Jacob said, *"Me have ye bereaved of my children: Joseph*

is not, and Simeon is not, and ye will take Benjamin away:
all these things are against me." He said Benjamin *"shall*
not go down with you; for his brother is dead, and he is left
alone: if mischief befall him by the way in the which ye go,
then shall ye bring down my gray hairs with sorrow to the
grave."

When their food was all gone they had no other
choice. The sons insisted that they would not go without Benjamin, because the Egyptian lord had said,
"Ye shall not see my face, except your brother be with
you." Judah offered, *"I will be surety for him; of my hand*
shalt thou require him: if I bring him not unto thee, and set
him before thee, then let me bear the blame for ever: For
except we had lingered, surely now we had returned this
second time" (Genesis 43:9, 10).

By force of necessity Jacob finally granted their
request. He sent a present for the man: of the best
fruit of the land, a little balm, a little honey, spices,
myrrh, nuts, almonds, and double money, saying,
"Take also your brother, and arise, go again unto the
man: And God Almighty give you mercy before the
man, that he may send away your other brother, and
Benjamin. If I be bereaved *of my children,* I am
bereaved." He never dreamed that Joseph, for whom
he had grieved for twenty years, would yet (as a type
of Christ) be the greatest benefactor for Jacob and his
whole family.

When Joseph saw his brothers, and Benjamin with
them, he commanded that they be brought to his

house to dine with him at noon. Before meeting Benjamin, he went into his chamber and wept. Then he washed his face, and with self-control requested that the meal be served. He had the men seated according to their ages, and sent servings to them from his own table: but Benjamin's serving was five times as much as any of theirs. He was testing their attitude toward Benjamin.

And he commanded the steward of his house, saying, Fill the men's sacks with food, as much as they can carry, and put every man's money in his sack's mouth. And put my cup, the silver cup, in the sack's mouth of the youngest, and his corn money. And he did according to the word that Joseph had spoken. As soon as the morning was light, the men were sent away, they and their asses. And when they were gone out of the city, and not yet far off, Joseph said unto his steward, Up, follow after the men; and when thou dost overtake them, say unto them, Wherefore have ye rewarded evil for good? Is not this it in which my lord drinketh, and whereby indeed he divineth? ye have done evil in so doing (Genesis 44:1-5).

Things had gone well, and the eleven brothers were on their way home, rejoicing. But the final discipline in God's *arm of correction* was still coming. Then came Joseph's steward, asking why they had rewarded evil for good in taking Joseph's silver cup. Confident of their innocence, they said, *"With whomsoever of thy servants it be found, both let him die, and we also will be my lord's bondmen.*" But the steward searched their bags, beginning with the oldest and finishing with the youngest. He found the cup in Benjamin's sack where he himself had put it!

Tearing their clothes, they returned to Joseph brokenhearted. And Judah, who had suggested selling Joseph to the Ishmaelites, made a long, heartbroken plea to let Benjamin go home to his father while Judah would stay as a bondman to Joseph.

When Joseph could no longer restrain himself, he cried, "*Cause every man to go out from me.*" Then Joseph made himself known to his brothers. He wept so loudly that the Egyptians and the house of Pharaoh heard. What will it be like when Christ reveals Himself to Israel "the *second* time."[3]

> *And Joseph said unto his brethren, Come near to me, I pray you. And they came near. And he said, I am Joseph your brother, whom ye sold into Egypt. Now therefore be not grieved, nor angry with yourselves, that ye sold me hither: for God did send me before you to preserve life. For these two years hath the famine been in the land: and yet there are five years, in the which there shall neither be earing nor harvest. And God sent me before you to preserve you a posterity in the earth, and to save your lives by a great deliverance. So now it was not you that sent me hither, but God: and he hath made me a father to Pharaoh, and lord of all his house, and a ruler throughout all the land of Egypt (Genesis 45:4-8).*

Instead of accusing his brothers for having sold him into Egypt, Joseph explained that God had sent him there to preserve their whole clan alive.

("At the *second time* Joseph was made known to his brethren; and Joseph's kindred was made known unto Pharaoh.[4] What will it be like when Jesus at His second coming reveals Himself to Israel?[5] That will be a great and profound revelation. Then, for the first time, not only apostate Israel, but all the *Pharaohs and kings* of the world will recognize Jesus for who He really is? Consider Psalm 2:1-12.)

From Preserver to Abundant Provider

He urged his brothers to hurry home, gather up their families, and bring them all to Egypt. He sent twenty donkeys loaded with corn, bread, and meat for the people, and wagons to bring them all. *"He gave each man changes of raiment; but to Benjamin he gave three hundred pieces of silver, and five changes of raiment"* (Genesis 45:22), foreshadowing God's benevolent grace. Furthermore, he cautioned them to travel peaceably.

When Jacob heard that Joseph was alive, and saw all the wagons and everything that Joseph had sent, his spirit revived, and he said, *"I will go and see him before I die."* Jacob and all his descendants started on their journey, but stopped at Beersheba to offer sacrifices unto God. There God met Jacob, confirming his decision to go to Egypt.

And he said, I am God, the God of thy father: fear not to go down into Egypt; for I will there make of thee a great nation: I will go down with thee into Egypt; and I will also surely bring thee up again: and Joseph shall put his hand upon thine eyes (Genesis 46:3, 4).

When Jacob's whole family arrived in Egypt, Pharaoh told Joseph to give them the area of Goshen, the best land that Egypt had to offer.

And Joseph placed his father and his brethren, and gave them a possession in the land of Egypt, in the best of the land, in the land of Rameses, as Pharaoh had commanded. And Joseph nourished his father, and his brethren, and all his father's household, with bread, according to their families (Genesis 47:11, 12).

Before the famine was over, the Egyptians had given their cattle, their land, and themselves to Pharaoh in exchange for food.[6] Likewise, this reminds us of the blessings of God promised to the believers. This is experienced only by those who have a blood-bought relationship with Jesus Christ.

Joseph Receives the Birthright

Joseph and his two sons, Manasseh and Ephraim, came to see Jacob. Naming the younger before the elder, Jacob said, *"Now thy two sons, Ephraim and Manasseh, . . . are mine; as Reuben and Simeon[7] are mine, and the issue, which thou begettest after them, shall be thine"* (Genesis 48:5, 6). Ephraim and Manasseh are therefore named among the twelve tribes of Israel, making up for the non-inheriting tribe of Levi, as well as giving Joseph a double inheritance (Deuteronomy 21:17).

Joseph brought his sons that Jacob might bless them. He placed them so that Jacob should lay his right hand on Manasseh's head and his left hand on Ephraim's head. But Jacob crossed his arms wittingly, laying his right hand on Ephraim's head. Joseph objected, saying,

> *Not so, my father: for this* [Manasseh] *is the first-born; put thy right hand upon his head. And his father refused, and said, I know it, my son, I know it: he also shall become a people, and he also shall be great: but truly his younger brother shall be greater than he, and his seed shall become a multitude of nations. And he blessed them that day, saying, In thee shall Israel bless, saying, God make thee as Ephraim and as Manasseh: and he set Ephraim before Manasseh* (Genesis 48:18b-20).

Thus Jacob gave the birthright to Joseph and made Ephraim, the second-born, superior to Manasseh.

When Jacob blessed all his sons before he died, he gave a major blessing to Joseph.[8] Only the blessing upon Judah,[9] through whom Christ came in the flesh, equaled and surpassed that of Joseph.

Forgiveness Overcomes Mistreatment

When Jacob had died and was buried, Joseph's

brothers who had so cruelly mistreated him in his youth, realized that now Joseph certainly had the power to avenge himself of their cruelties. They sent to him a messenger begging for mercy and pardon. When Joseph heard it, he wept. Joseph, being a multiple figure of Christ, had a power far greater than that of revenge. **He had power to forgive!** His brothers also came and fell down before his face, and said, *"Behold, we be thy servants."* But *"he comforted them, and spake kindly unto them"* (Genesis 50:15-21).

When Joseph as a teenager had those prophetic dreams,[10] his brothers hated and envied him intensely, *"and could not speak peaceably unto him."* But when those dreams were fulfilled, Joseph proved to be the greatest and most gracious human benefactor his brothers ever had. God worked wonders in the life of Joseph, as a human foreshadow of Jesus Christ, *"despised and rejected of men; a man of sorrows, and acquainted with grief"* (Isaiah 53:3), yet Jesus is the greatest and most gracious Benefactor the human race can ever know! Of Him it is said:

> *Wherefore God also hath highly exalted him [Jesus Christ], and given him a name which is above every name: That at the name of Jesus every knee should bow, of things in heaven, and things in earth, and things under the earth; And that every tongue should confess that Jesus Christ is Lord, to the glory of God the Father (Philippians 2:9-11).*

Questions for Consideration and Discussion

1. Was the colorful coat a blessing or a grief to Joseph?
2. What does that coat teach us about favoritism?
3. Did God's control make the selling of Joseph less sinful?
4. What in Joseph's life constituted his greatest trial?
5. What was his greatest victory?
6. What did God accomplish with Joseph in Egypt?
7. Why did Joseph wait so long to identify himself?
8. Why did Jacob claim Joseph's sons as his own?
9. Why did Jacob set Ephraim above Manasseh?
10. How many similarities can you find between Joseph and Christ?

---

1. Genesis 41
2. Luke 3:23
3. See Zechariah 12:10-14
4. Acts 7:13
5. Zechariah 12:9-14; 14:1-4
6. Genesis 47:14-26
7. Reuben and Simeon were Jacob's two oldest sons. But Reuben, by defilement (Genesis 35:22; 49:4) had lost his birthright, which Jacob here bestowed upon Joseph. (See also 1 Chronicles 5:1, 2).
8. Genesis 49:22-26
9. Genesis 49:8-12
10. Genesis 37:5-11

8

A Man Faithful in All God's House

My servant Moses . . . is faithful in all mine house
(Numbers 12:7; Hebrews 3:5).

Genesis closes with all Israel in Egypt, dwelling happily in the best of the land (Genesis 47:6, 11, 12), and highly favored by all the people. They were so favored not by virtues of their own, but because they were the family of Joseph, the renowned hero who had saved Egypt from the famine.

Then there arose a new king, knowing neither Joseph nor God (Exodus 1:8-12). He was like many of our legislators today, who seem to know nothing of the principles embraced by the founding fathers of our nation. This new king was a heartless monarch, inspired by Satan whose basic aim, ever since the fall of man, has been to destroy the race through whom God promised to send the Messiah. Pharaoh decreed that every Hebrew male was to be thrown into the river at birth (Exodus 1:22).

Into that hazardous setting Moses was born, not only as a Hebrew slave, but also, as it were, right into the jaws of death. But God is never outwitted or frustrated by enemies of any sort. Look what God wrought through the simple, trusting faith of those captive parents.

Forty Years of Royalty

By faith Moses, when he was born, was hid three months of his parents, because they saw he was a proper child;[1] and they were not afraid of the king's commandment (Hebrews 11:23).

When they could no longer hide the child, his mother took an ark of bulrushes and waterproofed it with pitch inside and outside, sealing it with care and prayer. She put the child into that ark and placed it between the flags at the edge of the very river in which Moses was sentenced to die. Miriam stood nearby to watch what would happen. No doubt his mother, Jochebed, was at home holding on to God with intense prayer for the child's life (Exodus 2:1-10).

Miriam came running, saying, "Mamma, Come quickly. Pharaoh's daughter wants our baby, and she wants you to nurse him for her!" God saw to it that Moses got the benefit of godly instruction from his parents before he was adopted into Pharoah's family. Then He watched him grow to manhood as an adopted son of Pharaoh's daughter, in the royal palace of the very king who had decreed his death. There he was *homeschooled,* with God as his *Supervisor.*

We have no evidence that Pharaoh had any sons. Many have assumed that Moses was heir to the throne, and was diligently trained in preparation for that position. Although he was *"learned in all the wisdom of the Egyptians"* (Acts 7:22), he never forgot the principles of faith he had learned from his parents. God always maintained headquarters in the *living room* of Moses' heart.

> *By faith Moses, when he was come to years, refused to be called the son of Pharaoh's daughter; Choosing rather to suffer affliction with the people of God, than to enjoy the pleasures of sin for a season; Esteeming the reproach of Christ greater riches than the treasures in Egypt: for he had respect unto the recompense of the reward (Hebrews 11:24-26).*

When Moses was grown he saw an Egyptian beating a Hebrew. Feeling an urge to deliver his own people, Moses slew the Egyptian (Exodus 2:11, 12). He assumed the Israelites would understand that through him God was going to deliver them, *"but they understood not"* (Acts 7:25). When Pharaoh heard it, he disinherited Moses, terminated his royal status and sought to kill him. Again, God had other plans and further training for His servant Moses.

Forty Years of Humility

But Moses fled from the face of Pharaoh, and dwelt in the land of Midian (Exodus 2:15b).

Apparently the time was not yet ripe for bringing Israel out of Egypt, and Moses was not yet prepared for the task. He was demoted from a mighty Egyptian prince to an ordinary refugee. In Midian he enrolled in the *seminary of God* out in the desert, for forty years of *basic training in shepherding*, far away from the pomp and pride of Egyptian royalty. In the fortieth year of his enrollment, he met with God at the burning bush for a review of his faith (Exodus 3:1-10).

God called to him out of the burning bush, identifying Himself as the God of Abraham, Isaac, and Jacob. He said, *"Come now, I will send you to Pharaoh to bring my people out of Egypt."* God assured him, *"I will be with you,"* and gave him four miraculous signs with which to convince the people that God had sent him. The premature ambition that Moses had felt forty years earlier was gone. Moses begged to be excused, saying,

> *Who am I, that I should go unto Pharaoh, and that I should bring forth the children of Israel out of Egypt? . . . They will not believe me. . . . I am not eloquent, . . . I am slow of speech, and slow of tongue (Exodus 3:11b; 4:1, 10).*

> *And the LORD said unto him, Who hath made man's mouth? or who maketh the dumb, or deaf, or the seeing, or the blind? have not I the LORD?* **Now therefore go, and I will be with thy mouth, and teach thee what thou shalt say** *(Exodus 4:11, 12).*

Moses continued with excuses until the LORD was angry with him. God even compromised and appointed Aaron to be his spokesman, saying, *"He shall be to thee instead of a mouth, and thou shalt be to him instead of God. And thou shalt take this rod in thine hand, wherewith* **thou** *shalt do signs. . . . Go, return into Egypt: for all the men are dead which sought thy life"* (Exodus 4:16, 17, 19).

Finally Moses yielded to God's request. Together with his wife and two sons, they set out toward Egypt. Still one more thing needed to be corrected before Moses was ready for the task. In Midian he had neglected the covenantal sign that God required under the Mosaic covenant. It spoke of a unique separation unto God even in the midst of a noncovenantal environment. The report is very brief, and lacking in details which I will not seek to supply.

> *And it came to pass by the way in the inn, that the LORD met him, and sought to kill him. Then Zipporah took a sharp stone, and cut off the foreskin of her son, and cast it at his feet, and said, Surely a bloody husband art thou to me. So he let him go: then she said, A bloody husband thou art, because of the circumcision (Exodus 4:24-26).*

Both forty-year periods of Moses' training came in two stages. The period in Egypt began with several years in the home of his godly parents, then continued in the royal palace. The period in Midian consisted of approximately forty years with God, in the sheepfolds of Jethro the priest of Midian, climaxed by the review at the burning bush and the final test in those few hours with God in a wayside inn. So Moses had eighty years of training for forty years of service. From then on he proved to be outstandingly loyal, as God Himself testified.

Forty Years of Loyalty

And the Lord *said to Aaron, Go into the wilderness to meet Moses. And he went, and met him in the mount of God, and kissed him. And Moses told Aaron all the words of the* Lord *who had sent him, and all the signs which he had commanded him. And Moses and Aaron went and gathered together all the elders of the children of Israel: And Aaron spake all the words which the* Lord *had spoken unto Moses, and did the signs in the sight of the people. And* **the people believed:** *and when they heard that the* Lord *had visited the children of Israel, and that he had looked upon their affliction, then they* **bowed their heads and worshipped** *(Exodus 4:27-31).*

Then the raging contest began. Pharaoh, inspired by Satan, determined to hold onto his slaves, just as God had said he would. The ten plagues that followed demonstrated God's judgment upon ten different gods of Egypt, and on those who worshipped them. The ten plagues primarily dealt with the Egyptians, so we will move on to see God working through Moses with His own chosen people, national Israel.

A. From Egypt to Sinai

If God had come to deliver Israel, why did He permit their cruel oppressors to so intensify their burdens? Even so, before they crossed the Red Sea, when they saw the Egyptian army pursuing them they murmured against Moses, saying, *"It had been better for us to serve the Egyptians, than that we should die in the wilderness"* (Exodus 14:12b). It must have been for their own good that God let them be driven so mercilessly at the very end of their bondage. It was time for them to be sick of Egypt and ready to be unconditionally committed to God.

The same God who had used the ten plagues to instruct and convict the Egyptians now used the Egyptian army to test Israel so that they would learn to trust in God. After leading Israel into what looked to them like an inescapable trap, God permitted the pursuing army to close the *trap* behind them. Then He led them in a miraculous delivery through the middle of the sea.

> *And Moses said unto the people, Fear ye not, stand still, and see the salvation of the LORD, which he will show to you to day: for the Egyptians whom ye have seen to day, ye shall see them again no more for ever. The LORD shall fight for you, and ye shall hold your peace (Exodus 14:13, 14).*

> *And the LORD said unto Moses, Wherefore criest thou unto me? speak unto the children of Israel, that they go forward: But lift thou up thy rod, and stretch*

out thine hand over the sea, and divide it: and the children of Israel shall go on dry ground through the midst of the sea. And I, behold, I will harden the hearts of the Egyptians, and they shall follow them: and I will get me honour upon Pharaoh, and upon all his host, upon his chariots, and upon his horsemen (Exodus 14:15-17).

When Moses lifted his rod as God directed, the sea opened up, and all Israel walked through on dry ground. God hardened the hearts of the Egyptians so that they followed. In the midst of the sea is where He had chosen to dispose of Pharaoh and his army. *"And the angel of God,[2] which went before the camp of Israel, removed and went behind them; and the pillar of the cloud went from before their face, and stood behind them"* (Exodus 14:19). God made sure that the army could not stop Israel. He even took off their chariot wheels, so that driving was extremely difficult (Exodus 14:25). A *drag race* at the bottom of the sea!

*And the waters returned, and covered the chariots, and the horsemen, and all the host of Pharaoh that came into the sea after them; there remained not so much as one of them. But the children of Israel walked upon dry land in the midst of the sea; and the waters were a wall unto them on their right hand, and on their left. Thus the LORD saved Israel that day out of the hand of the Egyptians; and Israel saw the Egyptians dead upon the sea shore. And Israel saw **that great work** which the LORD did upon the Egyp-*

tians: and the people feared the LORD, *and believed the* LORD, *and his servant Moses (Exodus 14:28-31).*

It was very appropriate for Moses and Israel to sing unto the LORD the song of victory as recorded in Exodus 15:1-19. **God's great work** with Israel was just beginning. God was now conditioning more than two million people to be *"a special people unto himself"* (Deuteronomy 7:6). Training and conditioning always requires a great deal of proving. And the desert through which they traveled was an excellent proving ground, both for Moses and the people.

Imagine traveling three days in a desert without water (Exodus 15:22-24), then finding the waters of Marah so bitter they could not drink them! Moses cried unto the Lord, and the Lord showed him a tree that would make the waters sweet. *"There he made for them a statute and an ordinance, and there he **proved them.**"*

> *And said, If thou wilt diligently hearken to the voice of the* LORD *thy God, and wilt do that which is right in his sight, and wilt give ear to his commandments, and keep all his statutes, I will put none of these diseases upon thee, which I have brought upon the Egyptians: for **I am the*** LORD ***that healeth thee** (Exodus 15:26).*

Their wilderness foreshadows the world in which we live. Today's world is increasingly hostile toward God and His people, just like their desert plagued Israel with many struggles and hard trials. Life and death without Christ are unbearably bitter, as typified by the waters of Marah. He sweetens the waters for all who fully trust in Him. To the Christian, life and death are both sweet when Christ is in us, and has control. Nothing else can give us victory over Satan, sin, and self.

By the grace of God, Israel's next move brought them to Elim, *"where were twelve wells of water, and seventy palm trees: and they encamped there by the waters"* (Exodus 15:27). God needs to be stern sometimes, but He is always kind and good. After severe testings, He frequently provides a refreshing pause, such as in this case.

Next they entered the wilderness of Sin, and there again they murmured against Moses and Aaron, saying,

> *Would to God we had died by the hand of the* LORD *in the land of Egypt, when we sat by the flesh pots, and when we did eat bread to the full; for ye have brought us forth into this wilderness, to kill this whole assembly with hunger (Exodus 16:3).*

> *Then said the* LORD *unto Moses, Behold, I will rain bread from heaven for you; and the people shall go out and gather a certain rate every day,* **that I may prove them,** *whether they will walk in my law, or no (Exodus 16:4).*

> *And they tempted God in their heart by asking meat for their lust. Yea, they spake against God; they said, Can God furnish a table in the wilderness (Psalm 78:18, 19)?*

*And it came to pass, that at even the quails came
up, and covered the camp: and in the morning the
dew lay round about the host. And when the dew
that lay was gone up, behold, upon the face of the
wilderness there lay a small round thing, as small as
the hoar frost on the ground. And when the children
of Israel saw it, they said one to another, It is manna:
for they wist not what it was. And Moses said unto
them, This is the bread which the LORD hath given
you to eat (Exodus 16:13-15).*

God meant for them to understand that they were
totally dependent upon Him for survival, and that
He will never let them down. For forty years He fed
them with manna. It was a balanced diet and a free
gift, replacing many trainloads and many millions of
dollars worth of ordinary food every week. Nothing
else could have matched its quantity, quality, or
economy. The manna itself marvelously typified
Christ in more than a dozen ways.

They pitched in Rephidim, where there was no
water. Again they murmured against Moses. Moses
asked, *"Why chide ye with me? wherefore do ye tempt the
LORD?"* God told Moses to smite the rock with his
rod, and when he did, the water flowed abundantly
(Exodus 17:6). Smiting the Rock in Horeb typified
Christ smitten at Calvary to offer Living Water for
the salvation of all true believers.

B. Israel at Mount Sinai

In the third month after leaving Egypt they came to Sinai, "and there Israel camped before the Mount" (Exodus 19:1, 2). For the next nine or ten months this was God's basic training camp, where He tested and proved His people collectively.

> *And the LORD said unto Moses, Go unto the people, and sanctify them today and tomorrow, and let them wash their clothes, and be ready against the third day: for the third day the LORD will come down in the sight of all the people upon mount Sinai (Exodus 19:10, 11).*

Here He gave them the Ten Commandments (Exodus 20:3-17), and the Mosaic Law in general. He promised to send His Angel to bring them into the Promised Land.

> *Behold, I send an Angel before thee, to keep thee in the way, and to bring thee into the place which I have prepared. Beware of him, and obey his voice, provoke him not; for he will not pardon your transgressions: **for my name is in him**. . . . For mine Angel shall go before thee, and bring thee in unto the Amorites, and the Hittites, and the Perizzites, and the Canaanites, the Hivites, and the Jebusites: and I will cut them off (Exodus 23:20, 21, 23).*

At Sinai God instructed them to build the Tabernacle,[3] prefiguring Christ and His church on earth.[4] But while Moses continued on the Mount, receiving instructions to build the Tabernacle and communing with God, the people *"corrupted themselves."* They persuaded Aaron to make a golden calf, which they worshipped more vigorously than they had worshipped God. For the first time God said to Moses, *"Let me alone, that my wrath may wax hot against them, and that I may consume them: and I will make of thee a great nation"* (Exodus 32:10). Now that offer tested Moses, but Moses felt more concern for God's glory than for his own. He earnestly besought the LORD to spare the people, and to preserve His great name (Exodus 32:11-13).

C. From Sinai to Kadesh

Exodus is a Book of Redemption. Leviticus was their Religious Service Manual. Numbers records their travels from Sinai to Canaan. It includes the tragic revolt when ten of the twelve spies gave an evil report. They were at the very border of the Promised Land, but refused to trust God for the take-over. In fact, they said, *"Let us make a captain, and let us return into Egypt"* (Numbers 13:28–14:4). Because of that rebellion, they had to wander in the wilderness for thirty-eight more years, until all the men of war (except Joshua and Caleb) were consumed,[5] before they could finally enter the land of promise.

> *And the LORD said unto Moses, How long will this people provoke me? and how long will it be ere they believe me, for all the signs which I have showed among them? I will smite them with the pestilence, and disinherit them, and will make of thee a greater nation and mightier than they (Numbers 14:11, 12).*

This was the second time God threatened to destroy them. Notice how Moses interceded (Numbers 14:13-19), and how God responded (Numbers 14:20-24). Next we find the rebellion of Korah, Dathan, and Abiram.[6] Korah was a Levite and a Kohathite who, along with two hundred and fifty princes, was not content with his service assignment at the tabernacle. They contended with Aaron for the priesthood, daring to offer incense. *"And there came out a fire from the LORD, and consumed the two hundred and fifty men that offered incense".[7]*

Moses and Aaron were descendants of Levi, Jacob's third son. Dathan and Abiram were Reubenites, descendants of Jacob's first-born son. They clamored for leadership as a *birthright* privilege. They were more belligerent than Korah, and rudely accused Moses of failure (Numbers 16:12-15). The earth opened up and swallowed them and all their families alive,[8] which suggests that their sin exceeded the sin of Korah. We also find that *"the children of Korah died not"* (Numbers 26:11).[9]

Numbers 16:20-22 and verses 41-45, records the third and fourth times that God threatened to consume that rebellious congregation in a moment. Each time Moses passed the test with flying colors, interceding for them with all his heart. In doing so, he typified Christ, the greatest Intercessor of all. Twice, Moses was assisted by Aaron.

D. Even the Most Loyal Are Subject to Error

Soon they lacked water again, chiding with Moses, saying, "Would God that we had died when our brethren died before the LORD!" They even scolded Moses for bringing them out of Egypt (Numbers 20:3-5). They came to the Rock in Kadesh, which typified Christ in a role different from that of the Rock in Horeb. This Rock typified Christ exalted and glorified at the right hand of the Father, *the position from which He now sends the Comforter* (John 16:7).

At Horeb God had said, "Take . . . *thy rod, wherewith thou smotest the river, . . . and thou shalt **smite** the rock."* At Kadesh he was commanded to take "*the rod, . . . from before the Lord*" (Numbers 20:8, 9), which was Aaron's rod that had budded to verify Aaron's high priesthood (Numbers 17:5), and was kept before the Lord in the Ark of the covenant (Numbers 17:10). He was to take **that rod** and **speak** to the rock (make a high priestly intercession), but he was not supposed to strike it. Moses did not strike with "*the rod,"* but with "*his rod*" (Numbers 20:11). He struck once, and nothing happened. He struck again, and the water came, in spite of his violation. God was on duty. By striking the Rock that typified the risen and glorified Christ, Moses had marred a type that was most precious to God. Therefore he could not enter the Promised Land. At that point God canceled the *passports* of both Moses and Aaron (Numbers 20:12). No leader, however great, can violate God's instructions without serious consequences.

"*Now the man Moses was very meek, above all the men which were upon the face of the earth*" (Numbers 12:3). But after nearly forty years of patient endurance, his meekness finally broke under the strain. He burst out, saying, "*Hear now, ye rebels; must we fetch you water out of this rock?*" (Numbers 20:10). Only God can bring water out of a rock, "*and that Rock was Christ*" (1 Corinthians 10:4). The Psalmist states it sympathetically and well:

> *They angered him also at the waters of strife, so that it went ill with Moses for their sakes: because they provoked his spirit, so that he spake unadvisedly with his lips* (Psalm 106:32, 33).

> *So Moses the servant of the LORD died there in the land of Moab, according to the word of the LORD (Deuteronomy 34:5).*

Except for his violation at the Rock in Kadesh, Moses verily was faithful in all his house as a servant (Hebrews 3:5; Numbers 12:7). Thirty-two times the Bible speaks of Moses as the servant of the LORD; servant of God; my servant; His servant, etc. In promising the coming of Christ, God said to Moses, "*I will raise them up a Prophet from among their brethren, **like unto thee**, . . .*" (Deuteronomy 18:18, 19). This shows that God considered Moses a foreshadowing of his great Successor, our Lord Jesus Christ.

Now all these things happened unto them for

ensamples: and they are written for our admonition,
upon whom the ends of the world are come (1 Corinthians 10:11).

And there arose not a prophet since in Israel like
unto Moses, whom the LORD knew face to face, in all
the signs and the wonders, which the LORD sent him
to do in the land of Egypt to Pharaoh, and to all his
servants, and to all his land, and in all that mighty
hand, and in all the great terror which Moses showed
in the sight of all Israel" (Deuteronomy 34:10-12).

Questions for Consideration and Discussion

1. Who really protected baby Moses in the basket?
2. How long do you think he was with his parents?
3. In fleeing from Pharaoh, what led him to Midian?
4. What did sheep contribute to his further training?
5. How long did Moses wait on Sinai before God
   spoke?
6. Who was the Angel of God that went with Israel?
7. How often did Moses fast for forty days and
   nights?
8. Why did they not enter Canaan the first time?
9. How did the Rock and rod at Kadesh differ from
   those at Horeb?
10. In what way was Moses like unto Christ (Deuter-
    onomy 18:18)?

---

1. Exceeding fair, Acts 7:20
2. The pre-incarnate Jehovah, Exodus 13:21; 14:24

3. The Author's book, *Seeing Christ in the Tabernacle,* discusses the typology of the tabernacle in more detail.

4. Exodus, chapters 25-40

5. Deuteronomy 2:14-18; Joshua 5:4-6

6. Numbers 16:1-11

7. Numbers 16:35

8. Numbers 16:31-34

9. Samuel (the man of God with three offices: prophet, priest, and judge) was a sixteenth generation descendant of Korah (compare 1 Samuel 8:2 with 1 Chronicles 6:33-37).

9

From Slavery to Chief Commander

And Moses said unto Joshua, Choose us out men, and go out, fight with Amalek (Exodus 17:9a).

At the commandment of the Lord, the children of Israel encamped at Rephidim, and there was no water for the people to drink (Numbers 17:1). It is a well-known fact that neither people, animals, nor plants can live without water. Again, God was testing Israel's faith in Him as their Provider. Instead of looking in faith to God who led them there, they rose up and murmured against Moses. By doing what God said, the smitten Rock in Horeb burst wide open, gushing forth a river of water clean and pure, as noted in the previous chapter.

"Then came Amalek, and fought with Israel in Rephidim" (Numbers 17:8). Moses abruptly, with no introduction, brought Joshua on the scene as commander of Israel's first army. Five months earlier these people were slaves in Egypt, making bricks and serv-

ing with rigor under the whips of cruel slave masters. Born and reared as a slave himself, Joshua had no experience in transforming slaves into soldiers who could repel the attack of an enemy. His reliance on God was more effective than experience would have been.

This was the first time Israel was required to fight a physical battle, yet it was also a spiritual battle. As long as Moses, watching from a hilltop, upheld the rod of God, *"Israel prevailed: and when he let down his hand, Amalek prevailed"* (Numbers 17:11). Thus Joshua defeated Amalek.

> *And the* Lord *said unto Moses, Write this* for *a memorial in a book, and rehearse* it *in the ears of Joshua: for I will utterly put out the remembrance of Amalek from under heaven. . . . For he said, Because the* Lord *hath sworn that the* Lord *will have war with Amalek from generation to generation (Exodus 17:14, 16).*

The Lord waging *"war with Amalek from generation to generation,"* typifies God at work in subduing man's carnal flesh from generation to generation. Eventually He *"will utterly put out the remembrance of Amalek from under heaven"* (Exodus 17:14).

Our next three glimpses of Joshua show him as Moses' minister,[1] the son of Nun,[2] zealously defending the leadership and honor of Moses (Numbers 11:28, 29).

Not until the twelve spies were sent to search the

land of Canaan do we learn that his name had been
Oshea/Hoshea,[3] meaning *deliverer*.[4] But at the sending of the spies, Moses renamed him *Jehoshua*,[5] meaning *Jehovah saves*. The name was then shortened to
Joshua, and with three exceptions is used that way
about two hundred times throughout the Bible.

The Greek rendering in the New Testament is *Jesus*
(Hebrews 4:8), obviously referring to Joshua. His
name, as well as his work, prefigured our Lord and
Saviour.

But why did they send spies? God had been their
constant guide ever since they left Egypt. He alone
knew every foot of the ground they were to cover.

God had promised:

> *I will send my fear before thee, and will destroy all
> the people to whom thou shalt come, and I will make
> all thine enemies turn their backs unto thee. And I
> will send hornets before thee, which shall drive out
> the Hivite, the Canaanite, and the Hittite, from before
> thee (Exodus 23:27, 28).*

Moses explained the situation:

> *And when we departed from Horeb, we went
> through all that great and terrible wilderness, which
> ye saw by the way of the mountain of the Amorites,
> as the LORD our God commanded us; and we came to
> Kadeshbarnea.   And I said unto you, Ye are come
> unto the mountain of the Amorites, which the LORD
> our God doth give unto us.   Behold, the LORD thy
> God hath set the land before thee: go up and possess*

it, as the LORD *God of thy fathers hath said unto thee; fear not, neither be discouraged" (Deuteronomy 1:19-21).*

And ye came near unto me every one of you, and said, We will send men before us, and they shall search us out the land, and bring us word again by what way we must go up, and into what cities we shall come. And the saying pleased me well: and I took twelve men of you, one of a tribe: and they turned and went up into the mountain . . . and searched it out (Deuteronomy 1:22-24).

Instead of believing God and trusting Him, they chose to put confidence in men. Ten of their twelve spies went by sight, not by faith. Seeing giants, they forgot about God. They said, *"the land eats up the inhabitants thereof; and all the people that we saw in it are men of great stature. We were in our own sight as grasshoppers, and so we were in their sight"* (Numbers 13:32b, 33b). But Joshua and Caleb, led by another Spirit, rent their clothes and said:

If the LORD *delight in us, then he will bring us into this land, and give it us; a land which floweth with milk and honey. Only rebel not ye against the* LORD, *neither fear ye the people of the land; for they are bread for us: their defence is departed from them, and the* LORD *is with us: fear them not (Numbers 14:8-9).*

Only two years after leaving Egypt, they were at the very edge of the Promised Land, with the wilderness journey behind them and the promise of God before them. Over and over God had proved Himself ever so faithful and trustworthy, as Joshua and Caleb testified.

> *But all the congregation bade stone them with stones. And the glory of the* LORD *appeared in the tabernacle of the congregation before all the children of Israel (Numbers 14:10).*

> *And the* LORD *spake unto Moses and unto Aaron, saying, How long shall I bear with this evil congregation, which murmur against me? . . . As truly as I live, saith the* LORD*, as ye have spoken in mine ears, so will I do to you: Your carcasses shall fall in this wilderness; and* [your men of war] *. . . shall not come into the land, . . . save Caleb . . . and Joshua . . . (Numbers 14:26-30).*

> *But your little ones, which ye said should be a prey, them will I bring in, and they shall know the land which ye have despised. . . . And your children shall wander in the wilderness forty years, and bear your whoredoms, until your carcasses be wasted in the wilderness. . . . and ye shall know my breach of promise* [or, "you shall know My rejection," NKJV. "That you may know what it is when I withdraw my hand," Luther's German] *(Numbers 14:31-34).*

Because of this rebellion, they had to retreat and wander another thirty-eight years in the wilderness. They had to wait until all the men of war, except Joshua and Caleb, had died.[6]

Moses, representing the law, was God's chosen man to lead them out of bondage, to guide them through the wilderness, and to teach them good discipline. Twice, thirty-eight years apart, Moses had brought Israel to the very border of the land, but he could not bring them in. The first time, his people rebelled. The second time, thirty-eight years later, Moses himself had erred by striking the rock at the water of Meribah (Numbers 20:7-13). Therefore, Moses could not bring God's people over the Jordan into the Promised Land.

Joshua Did What Moses Could Not Do

Herein is a lesson we need to understand. What Moses did needed to be done, and he did it well. Without discipline and obedience, discipleship is impossible. But as imperative as discipline is, that alone cannot bring salvation. Only Joshua [meaning, **Jehovah saves**] could take Israel across the Jordan, into the Promised Land.

Wherefore the law was our schoolmaster [disciplinarian[7]] *to bring us unto Christ, that we might be justified by faith (Galatians 3:24).*

When God had laid Moses to rest, He said to Joshua,

Moses my servant is dead; now therefore arise, go over this Jordan, thou, and all this people, unto the land which I do give to them, even to the children of Israel. Every place that the sole of your foot shall tread upon, that have I given unto you, as I said unto Moses. From the wilderness and this Lebanon even unto the great river, the river Euphrates, all the land of the Hittites, and unto the great sea toward the going down of the sun, shall be your coast. There shall not any man be able to stand before thee all the days of thy life: as I was with Moses, so I will be with thee: I will not fail thee, nor forsake thee. Be strong and of a good courage: for unto this people shalt thou divide for an inheritance the land, which I sware unto their fathers to give them (Joshua 1:2-6).

And Joshua rose early in the morning; and they removed from Shittim, and came to Jordan, he and all the children of Israel, and lodged there before they passed over (Joshua 3:1).

It was the time of the year when the Jordan overflowed all its banks. The waters did not part until the feet of the priests who bore the Ark were dipped into the edge of the water. Then the water that flowed down from the north *"stood and rose up upon an heap,"* while all the water from that spot flowed on south, leaving the river bed dry for Israel to cross over.

And the priests that bare the ark of the covenant of the Lord *stood firm on **dry ground** in the midst of Jordan, and all the Israelites passed over on **dry ground**, until all the people were passed clean over Jordan (Joshua 3:17).*

On the tenth day of the first month they passed over Jordan and encamped in Gilgal. Then and there they circumcised all the males that were born in the last forty years, for all the people that were born in the wilderness had not been circumcised (Joshua 5:3-5). That was an act of faith. What Simeon and Levi had done to the Shechemites[8] is proof that for several days Israel would not be in physical condition to cope with a possible attack from the Canaanites.

Circumcision of the flesh symbolized the removal of sin, which God must do for us in preparation for heaven. Even so, they needed that foreshadowing in preparation to inherit Canaan, their earthly Promised Land. In New Testament times Christians "are circumcised with the [spiritual] circumcision made without hands, in the putting off of the body of the sins of the flesh by the circumcision of Christ" (Colossians 2:11).

Israel encamped in Gilgal and kept the passover on the fourteenth day of Abib, "*at even in the plains of Jericho.*" The day after passover they ate "of the old corn of the land," and the next day the manna ceased. For forty years they had lived on a day by day supply of manna, but that day brought a permanent change of diet: they ate of the fruit of the land, just like everybody else.

Their victorious campaign to take possession of the land began with the miraculous taking of Jericho (Joshua 6:1-21). God, through Joshua, demonstrated unusual military tactics. Simply marching around the city once a day for six days, and seven times on the seventh day, then giving a shout as God had said, brought those massive walls down flat. Then they utterly destroyed every man, woman, and child, except Rahab and her family. Rahab evidently converted to faith in God, and became the great-great-grandmother of King David (Matthew 1:5, 6).

Achan's secret violation at Jericho resulted in unexpected defeat at the little city of Ai (Joshua 7:1-26). The incident proved to them that unbroken victory requires strict obedience. As long as Israel served the LORD and did what He required of them, it mattered not how many nations joined together against them. The Lord delivered every enemy into Israel's hand.

But Joshua, like Moses, made one unfortunate mistake. God had emphatically told them,

> *When the LORD thy God shall bring thee into the land whither thou goest to possess it, and hath cast out many nations before thee, . . . seven nations greater and mightier than thou; And when the LORD thy God shall deliver them before thee; thou shalt smite them, and utterly destroy them; thou shalt make no covenant with them, nor show mercy unto them: Neither shalt thou make marriages with them; thy daughter thou shalt not give unto his son, nor his daughter shalt thou take unto thy son. For they will turn away thy son from following me, that they may serve other gods: so will the anger of the LORD be kindled against you, and destroy thee suddenly (Deuteronomy 7:1-4).*

The Gibeonites, however, deceived Joshua. With old sacks, old shoes, ragged clothing, and moldy bread, they pretended to have come from a distant country. They said everything was new, and that the bread was taken hot from the oven when they started on their long journey. They hastened to make peace with Israel before Joshua discovered who they really were. And Joshua, without seeking counsel from the LORD (Joshua 9:14), made a treaty with them to let them live. Three days later they learned that these people were natives of Canaan, whom God had sentenced to be annihilated.

However, after they had sworn to a treaty,[9] that they had been warned not to make, God held them responsible for it. It became binding in heaven, in keeping with Matthew 18:18. More than 450 years later,[10] when King Saul violated that commitment, the LORD penalized Israel with three successive years of famine (2 Samuel 21:1).

Agreeing to spare the Gibeonites may have set a pattern toward sparing others as well. Judah "could not drive out the inhabitants of the valley;" "Benjamin did not drive out the Jebusites;" Manasseh spared the inhabitants of five different cities; Ephraim, Zebulun, Asher, Naphtali and Dan all spared people whom God had sentenced for destruction (Judges 1:19-35). And God said,

> *Else if ye do in any wise go back, and cleave unto*
> *the remnant of these nations, even these that remain*

among you, and shall make marriages with them, and
go in unto them, and they to you: Know for a cer-
tainty that the LORD *your God will no more drive out*
any of these nations from before you; but they shall be
snares and traps unto you, and scourges in your sides,
and thorns in your eyes, until ye perish from off this
good land which the LORD *your God hath given you*
(Joshua 23:12, 13).

That is exactly what happened. Disobedience
brought defeat. Israel did evil in the sight of the LORD,
intermarried with those who dwelt among them, and
served the gods of nations that God had commanded
them to totally destroy. Repeatedly, God gave them
up into the hands of their enemies, until they cried
unto the LORD and repented. When they repented,
He sent them a deliverer, but when the deliverer died,
they soon apostatized again. The Book of Judges
records seven cycles of apostasy.[11]

The conquest of Canaan symbolized victory over
the self-life. Violations by neglect brought costly
defeats and many sorrows. So it is with our personal
lives as well. We must confess, as did Jeremiah, "*O*
LORD, *I know that the way of man is not in himself: it is not*
in man that walketh to direct his steps" (Jeremiah 10:23).
A self-directed and self-centered life always makes a
sad, sad story. Without faith in Christ Jesus, man can
neither live victoriously nor be saved in the end.

Before Joshua died, he called the elders and officers of Israel together and pled with them to put away

the gods that their fathers had served east of the Euphrates, and in Egypt. *"And the people said unto Joshua, The LORD our God will we serve, and his voice will we obey"* (Joshua 24:24). He made a covenant with them, wrote their words in a book, and set up a great stone as a witness of their commitment (Joshua 24:20-28).

Joshua, the servant of the Lord, died at the age of one hundred ten. To the credit of his influence we are told that *"Israel served the LORD all the days of Joshua, and all the days of the elders that overlived Joshua, and which had known all the works of the LORD, that he had done for Israel"* (Joshua 24:31).

We don't know why there was no leader appointed to succeed him. Whatever the reason, four times the Book of Judges mentions, with a note of sadness, that *"in those days there was no king in Israel, but every man did that which was right in his own eyes."*[12] Even God's people need faithful leadership. *"Whatsoever things were written aforetime were written for our learning."* May we learn our lessons well.

Questions for Consideration and Discussion

1. What are some ideal virtues we can learn from Joshua?
2. Why did Moses change Oshea's name to Joshua (Numbers 13:16)?
3. What does the Bible say Joshua was full of?
4. What does the pillar in the midst of Jordan represent?

5. Why did they carry stones from Jordan to Gilgal?
6. What act of faith did Joshua do immediately at Gilgal?
7. How could he have avoided deception by the Gibeonites?
8. How did he respond to their defeat at Ai?
9. How many Kings did Joshua defeat in Canaan?
10. What was his final commitment and challenge to Israel?

---

1. Exodus 24:13; Joshua 1:1
2. Exodus 33:11
3. Numbers 13:8; Deuteronomy 32:44
4. Strong's Concordance
5. Numbers 13:16; 1 Chronicles 7:27
6. Numbers 14:26-34; Deuteronomy 2:14-16; Joshua 5:4, 6
7. Luther's German Translation
8. Genesis 34:25-29
9. Joshua 9:15
10. Acts 13:20
11. Judges 3:5–13:1
12. Judges 17:6; 18:1; 19:1; 21:25

10

Pagan Women Sanctified and Honored

For as the woman is of the man, even so
is the man also by the woman;
*but **all things of God***
(1 Corinthians 11:12).

Christ, who in eternity past had always been in the **form of God,**[1] emptied Himself of His divine prerogatives and took on, *not sinful flesh,* but *"the likeness of sinful flesh"* (Romans 8:3) for the express purpose of dying for all who receive Him by faith. All the women, including harlots, in His genealogy, were in need of, and eligible for, salvation through Christ.

Jesus is the only person **ever** to have any part in choosing His genealogy. We are amazed and humbled by some of His choices. Scattered through His genealogy are some whom we might be embarrassed to claim as ancestors. He claimed them freely, and their names are recorded in God's Word for everyone to see. If ever you feel righteous, beware! Jesus did not die for *the righteous,* but for sinners.

Men, as heads of the race, are responsible for the protection of women,[2] and should never stoop to the abuse of women. But too often they tend to be more critical of sinful women than of their own sins. For example, the scribes and Pharisees brought to Jesus a woman taken *in the very act of adultery* (John 8:4). How strange. It was impossible for her to commit adultery *alone*. Where was the guilty man? Was he one of the men who brought the woman?

Amnon, a son of David, is another example (2 Samuel 13). He alone was guilty, and extremely brutal. Then his lust, which he had mistaken for love, immediately turned into extreme hatred. His sister Tamar was totally innocent and helpless, but she suffered painful consequences.

In this chapter we are taking note of four women named in the genealogy of Jesus. They were all sinners. Some may have been victims of male abusiveness. All of them were in need of Jesus, by whom they were saved, sanctified, and honored.

I. Tamar, the Mother of Pharez
Genesis 38:1-30

Tamar, by no choice of her own, was born a Canaanite. Canaanites were descendants of Ham, and were never noted as a highly reputable people. Prior to the law, however, they were never officially labeled as *Not Recommended*.

Judah, the fourth son of Jacob, took a Canaanite

woman who bore him three sons: Er, Onan, and Shelah. When Er was grown, Judah took for him a Canaanite wife named Tamar. Er *"was wicked in the sight of the LORD; and the LORD slew him."* He died childless. The Levirate law required that his brother Onan take her to raise up seed for Er (Deuteronomy 25:5), which Onan determined to prevent, and he also died. So the family of Judah was not a very reputable family.

Judah told Tamar to remain a widow in her father's house until Shelah was grown. Shelah grew up, and Tamar was kept waiting in vain. Judah did not keep his promise. Furthermore, after Judah's wife died, Tamar put away her widow's garb, veiled her face and body to look like a harlot, and sat by the wayside where Judah would be passing by. It worked. He solicited her illicit service, for which she obtained his signet, bracelets, and staff, for future identification.

Three months later Judah learned that Tamar had played the harlot and was expecting a child. Judah said, *"Bring her forth and let her be burnt"* (Genesis 38:24). She displayed the signet, bracelets, and staff, which revealed the male participant in the affair. That saved her life. Then and there Judah confessed his sin and admitted, *"She hath been more righteous than I; because that I gave her not to Shelah my son."*

Tamar gave birth to twins, Pharez and Zarah, involving interesting typology beyond the intent of this writing (Genesis 38:27-30). Tamar is the first woman named in the New Testament along with her twins (Matthew 1:3). The three names are spelled slightly different from the Genesis account, and Zarah, although not a progenitor, is inserted as a brother. He is the only person so honored in the genealogy. That, too, adds interest to the study!

The Scriptures in no way condone the sins of Judah or Tamar. The accounts are recorded as a warning to all of us, but especially to the praise and glory of Jesus Christ, who makes salvation possible for all who seek it by grace through faith.

II. The Harlot Rahab

By faith the harlot Rahab perished not with them that believed not, when she had received the spies with peace (Hebrews 11:31).

In spite of the sinful profession in which Rahab had lived before she had sufficient knowledge of the God of Israel, she developed faith in God by what she heard concerning Israel. Observe her confession to the two spies Joshua had sent.

And she said unto the men, I know that the Lord hath given you the land, and that your terror is fallen upon us, and that all the inhabitants of the land faint because of you. For we have heard how the Lord dried up the water of the Red sea for you, when ye came out of Egypt; and what ye did unto the two kings of the Amorites, that were on the other side Jordan, Sihon and Og, whom ye utterly destroyed. And as soon as

*we had heard these things, our hearts did melt, nei-
ther did there remain any more courage in any man,
because of you: for the LORD your God, he is God
in heaven above, and in earth beneath (Joshua
2:9-11).*

This confession and Hebrews 11:31 convince me
that Rahab had converted from harlotry to a saving
faith in God, and that by faith she was cleansed from
her former life of sin. That is the kind of people Jesus
came to save. He gladly gave her the honor of being
named in His genealogy. A saved and sanctified sinner is always a shining token of God's redeeming
grace. But a boasting, self-righteous church member
is always a reproach to the name of Christ as well as
to His church.

III. Ruth the Moabitess

*An Ammonite or Moabite shall not enter into the
congregation of the LORD; even to their tenth generation shall they not enter into the congregation of the
LORD for ever" (Deuteronomy 23:3).*

That was God's pronouncement against Moab
upon the tragedy of Baal-peor. Balaam, when he
could not curse Israel, counseled the Moabites to
seduce Israel by luring them into adultery and idolatry. This had devastating effects, from which twenty-
four thousand Israelites died of the plague.[3]

Some 275 years later, during the time of the Judges,
there was a famine in Israel. Elimelech and Naomi

with their two sons, Mahlon and Chilion, went to sojourn in the land of Moab. Before long, Elimelech died. Naomi and her sons, however, continued there about ten years. The sons both married women of Moab. Mahlon married Ruth and Chilion married Orpah, but both men also died, leaving the three widows to suffer alone.

The famine in Israel had ended, and Naomi yearned to return to Bethlehem. Ruth and Orpah had both started out with her, until Naomi advised them to stay in Moab with their own people. As they considered and weighed their options, the three lifted up their voices and wept. Orpah decided to retain her Moabite faith. She kissed Naomi farewell and went *"back unto her people, and unto her gods"* —gods that could neither think nor move, and could never save a soul!

Ruth studied more deeply. Looking beyond the here and now, beyond what eyes could see and hands could touch, she made a decision with eternal dimensions. She said, *"Thy people shall be my people, and thy God my God: where thou diest, will I die, and there will I be buried: the LORD do so to me, and more also, if ought but death part thee and me"* (Ruth 1:16b,17). She not only chose to be a spititual Israelitess, but she chose the God of Israel instead of the gods of Moab.

What about the ban pronounced against all Moabites in Deuteronomy 23:3? Did not wives inherit the status of their husbands? (For example, see

Bathsheba below.) Moreover, God rebuked Miriam and Aaron for accusing Moses *"because of the Ethiopian woman whom he had married"* (Numbers 12:1). More importantly, Ruth's spiritual transformation lifted her above the national rejection of her people. God welcomed her on the basis of her commitment, confirmed by her character. He gave her a wonderful husband in the person of Boaz. She became a great-grandmother of King David and is registered in the genealogy of Jesus. She was truly sanctified and is highly honored.

IV. Bathsheba, the Former Wife of Uriah the Hittite

But thou shalt utterly destroy them; namely, *the Hittites, and the Amorites, the Canaanites, and the Perizzites, the Hivites, and the Jebusites; as the* LORD *thy God hath commanded thee (Deuteronomy 20:17).*

Bathsheba was the daughter of Eliam (2 Samuel 11:3), the son of Ahithophel (2 Samuel 23:34), but had officially become a Hittite by her marriage to Uriah. The Hittites were one of those nations that the Lord had designated for total destruction, even before banning the Moabites. Those who remained in Israel were left because of Israel's disobedience (Judges 2:1-3; 3:5-7).

We are left to wonder about Bathsheba's indecent exposure that ignited David's passions on the evening of his infamous transgression (2 Samuel 11:2). David of course incurred the greater guilt, but she had lighted the flame by which David was *carried away* by his own lusts. If she had been as discreet as Vashti (Esther 1:10-12), both could have been spared from the tragic sin that led on to the plotted murder of Uriah. What a fire a little spark may kindle!

The Lord sent the prophet Nathan who jolted David with an eye-opening parable, and some long-term consequences affecting his family. Then he added, *"The LORD also hath put away thy sin; thou shalt not die. Howbeit, because by this deed thou hast given great occasion to the enemies of the LORD to blaspheme, the child also that is born unto thee shall surely die"* (2 Samuel 12:13b, 14). We are glad for David's humble confession and for the depth of his penitence, manifested by the following Psalms:

> *When I kept silence, my bones waxed old through my roaring all the day long. For day and night thy hand was heavy upon me: my moisture is turned into the drought of summer. Selah. I acknowledged my sin unto thee, and mine iniquity have I not hid. I said, I will confess my transgressions unto the LORD; and thou forgavest the iniquity of my sin. Selah (Psalm 32:3-5).*

> *Have mercy upon me, O God, according to thy lovingkindness: according unto the multitude of thy tender mercies blot out my transgressions. Wash me thoroughly from mine iniquity, and cleanse me from my sin. For I acknowledge my transgressions: and my sin is ever before me (Psalm 51:1-3).*

Although we read nothing of Bathsheba's contrition, we trust that her tears blended with those of her husband. Their first child died as the Lord had said he would, but in due time He gave them another son named Solomon, of whom it is written, *"The LORD loved him"* (2 Samuel 12:24).

We are sure God also loved David and Bathsheba in spite of the family problems they suffered as a result of their sin. Their names are both included in the genealogy of Jesus (Matthew 1:6). From Proverbs 31:1, many assume that Bathsheba was the mother who taught *"king Lemuel"* the words of that chapter. At any rate, we trust that she became a godly and dedicated mother, entrusted with a son who actually had "the wisdom of Solomon."

Questions for Consideration and Discussion

1. What was required for progenitors of Jesus?
2. What about Tamar's native tribe and people?
3. What qualified her to join the tribe of Judah?
4. Who led Joshua's spies to Rahab's house? Why?
5. What evidence of faith did Rahab reveal?
6. What special purpose may God have had for Rahab?
7. What qualified Ruth to be a progenitor?
8. Name some personal qualities found in Ruth.
9. What personal responsibilities did Bathsheba violate?

10. What evidence of godliness do you see in her later
    life?

---

1. Philippians 2:6
2. 1 Corinthians 11:1-16
3. Numbers 25

11

From Obscurity to God's Hall of Fame

*The LORD hath sought him a man
after his own heart, and . . . commanded him
to be captain over his people
(1 Samuel 13:14b).*

A Humble Background

According to the Biblical record, God had told Samuel about His unnamed replacement for Saul before David was born. If King Saul reigned for forty years[1] and David was only thirty when he succeeded Saul,[2] then Saul had reigned ten years before David's birth. And the time charts that I have put twenty to thirty years between that revelation to Samuel and David's anointing in 1 Samuel 16.

God apparently designed that David's birthplace, early social status, occupation, persecution, and his final preeminence should foreshadow Christ's condescension to a lowly life style, His ministry on earth, and His final reign as King of Kings and Lord of lords. David was prenatally chosen of God, but (like Jesus)

131

was spared from popularity until he was fully grown.

We are first introduced to David as a teenager when God sent Samuel to Bethlehem to anoint one of the sons of Jesse. Samuel **went secretly for fear of Saul.** *"And he sanctified Jesse and his sons, and called them to the sacrifice"*—all but David. No one even thought of bringing in their little shepherd boy.

When Samuel saw the oldest son Eliab, he thought this was the one, but God "refused him." Jesse's seven older sons had all been sanctified, and all passed before Samuel in chronological order, but God had not chosen any of them.

Samuel asked Jesse, *"Are these all thy children?"*

Jesse answered, *"There remaineth yet the youngest, and, behold, he keepeth the sheep."*

Samuel responded, *"Send and fetch him: for we will not sit down till he come hither."*

When David arrived, the Lord said, *"Arise, anoint him: for this is he."*

> *Then Samuel took the horn of oil, and anointed him in the midst of his brethren: and the spirit of the LORD came upon David from that day forward. So Samuel rose up, and went to Ramah (1 Samuel 16:13).*

Apparently his anointing was kept secret for a long time. David was not thrust into popularity by the anointing, but by his musical and poetical skills, his victory over Goliath, and his abilities as a captain in Saul's army. His reign did not begin until years later— after Saul's death.

David and Goliath

Israel was at war with the Philistines, intimidated daily by the boastful threats of Goliath, the giant (1 Samuel 17: 4-11, 16). Jesse's three oldest sons were with Saul's army, and Jesse sent David to *"carry ten cheeses unto the captain of their thousand,"* and to see how his brothers were faring. And as he talked with them, Goliath again came on the scene, saying, *"I defy the armies of Israel this day; give me a man that we may fight together."* For forty days he had challenged Israel morning and evening with those words, but Saul and all Israel were greatly afraid.

David was alarmed—not by Goliath's threat, but by the cowardice of Israel. He exclaimed, *"Who is this uncircumcised Philistine, that he should defy the armies of the living God?"* (1 Samuel 17:26). David, more concerned for God's honor than for his own safety, volunteered to fight Goliath. Saul saw that as an impossible venture. David explained how a lion had snatched a lamb from his father's flock, and how he had gone after him, caught him by the beard and killed him. At another time a bear had done the same, and he had killed the bear. He assured Saul that the same God who delivered him from the lion and the bear would most assuredly deliver this God-defying Philistine into his hand as well (1 Samuel 17:32-37).

Finally, Saul agreed to let him go, but first he fitted him with weapons and armor. David put them off, saying, *"I cannot go with these; for I have not proved them"*

(1 Samuel 17:39). Equipped only with his staff, his sling, five smooth stones, and an unshakable faith in God, David went and with one stone felled this towering giant (9 feet, 9 inches tall). Read it all in 1 Samuel 17:4-51.

David and King Saul

David's battle with Goliath was over in a few minutes, but the conflict with King Saul lasted many years. Saul did not yet know that David was already anointed to be king of Israel. After the slaying of Goliath, Saul hailed David as a hero, and set him over his men of war. However, when the women celebrated David's victory, singing about Saul having *"slain his thousands, and David his ten thousands,"* Saul's jealousy seethed with rage. He said, *"And what can he have more but the kingdom? And Saul eyed David from that day forward"* (1 Samuel 18:7-8).

The next day the evil spirit from God came upon Saul, and David played for him as at other times. Saul threw his javelin, aiming to smite David to the wall with it. Twice David avoided Saul's attempt to kill him. Saul became afraid of David, because the LORD was with David, and was departed from Saul (1 Samuel 18:11, 12). *"And Saul became David's enemy continually"* (1 Samuel 18:29b). He made David captain over a thousand, and gave him his daughter Michal to wife, but in every move his admitted plot was to have David killed by the Philistines.

Four times in 1 Samuel 18 we are told that David *"behaved himself wisely . . . wisely in all his ways . . . very wisely . . . more wisely than all the servants of Saul."* Saul's son Jonathan loved David, and appealed to Saul in behalf of David. *"And Saul hearkened* [temporarily] *unto the voice of Jonathan: and Saul sware, As the* LORD *liveth, he shall not be slain"* (1 Samuel 19:6). In spite of his oath, just four verses later Saul again *"sought to smite David even to the wall with the javelin."* David slipped away, leaving the javelin stuck in the wall, and David fled and escaped that night. Obviously God was at work in David's life, and Satan was at work in Saul.

Three times[3] Saul sent messengers to kill David, or else bring him to Saul so that he could kill him. David told Jonathan, *"There is but a step between me and death."* Saul's anger was kindled against Jonathan, so that he tried to strike him with the javelin. Reversing his former oath, Saul declared to Jonathan that David *"shall surely die."*

Saul, with an army of *"three thousand chosen men out of all Israel"* (1 Samuel 24:2), pursued David *"as one doth hunt a partridge in the mountains"* (1 Samuel 26:20), determined to kill him. Thus the sad story continues to the end of Saul's life, vividly illustrating the fate of jealousy and departure from God.

Out of respect for Saul's office, David tolerated his abusiveness. Twice the Lord gave Saul into David's hands,[4] but David refused to lay his hand upon him, or to let his men do him any harm. Rather than harming Saul when he could have replaced him, David simply fled the country and sought refuge among the Philistines. Once he feigned madness to disguise himself, and several times he resorted to lies in self-defense. He did not seek the crown for which he was anointed years before, but waited patiently for the Lord to bring him to the throne, which God did in His own appointed time.

David as King

David was not a sinless king. He definitely violated God's command that Israel's king should not multiply wives to himself.[5] While he reigned at Hebron, he had six sons born from six different wives (2 Samuel 3:2-5). While he reigned at Jerusalem, David took more concubines and wives.[6] Worst of all was his sin of adultery with Bathsheba, and then plotting the death of her husband (2 Samuel 11:2-15). Of this sin he repented thoroughly. Psalms 32 and 51 describe his penitence.

Saul had the honor of being the first king of Israel, and Solomon's ivory throne overlaid with gold, and his world-wide fame, certainly exceeded the throne and fame of David. Yet *the throne of David* is a phrase that occurs eleven times: sometimes in a historical setting, sometimes in a prophetic setting. But *the throne of Saul,* or *the throne of Solomon,* are phrases I do not find in the Bible. Why not? What makes David's significance so lasting?

The greatest significance of **David's throne** was not his own personal reign, but its symbolic and prophetic character. David typified His great and final Successor, Jesus Christ the King of kings. Jesus is never called by the name of His other ancestors, such as the son of Jesse, or of Nathan, or of Hezekiah, or even Son of Abraham. But He is called the **Son of David** fifteen times in the synoptic Gospels. Nor is Jesus ever said to sit on the throne of Hezekiah, or Solomon, or any other of His royal ancestors, but He is promised the throne of David.

> *Of the increase of his government and peace there shall be no end, **upon the throne of David, and upon his kingdom,** to order it, and to establish it with judgment and with justice from henceforth even for ever. The zeal of the LORD of hosts will perform this (Isaiah 9:7).*

David lived very little beyond 70 years, but the throne of David was established before the Lord for ever.[7] More than three hundred years after David's death, Jeremiah, Ezekiel, and Hosea all prophesied of a **Greater David, the One** in whom the *throne of David* will be established forever.

> *Alas! for that day is great, so that none is like it: it is even the time of Jacob's trouble; but he shall be saved out of it. For it shall come to pass in that day, saith the LORD of hosts, that I will break his yoke from off thy neck, and will burst thy bonds, and strangers shall*

no more serve themselves of him: but they shall serve the LORD *their God, and* **David their king,** *whom I will raise up unto them (Jeremiah 30:7-9).*

Therefore will I save my flock, and they shall no more be a prey; and I will judge between cattle and cattle. And I will set up one shepherd over them, and he shall feed them, even **my servant David:** *he shall feed them, and he shall be their shepherd. And I the* LORD *will be their God, and* **my servant David** *a prince among them; I the* LORD *have spoken it (Ezekiel 34:22-24).*

Afterward shall the children of Israel return, and seek the LORD *their God, and* **David their king;** *and shall fear the* LORD *and his goodness* **in the latter days** *(Hosea 3:5).*

A Man After God's Heart

David was a man after God's own heart, not by virtue of an untainted record, but by virtue of his open and honest confessions, true repentance, and total reliance upon and profound reverence toward God. He never made excuses nor justified himself in his sins, but willingly accepted God's corrective discipline and glorified God for all His mercy. Notice the penitent tone of his confession and prayer:

(A Psalm of David, when Nathan the prophet came unto him, after he had gone in to Bathsheba.) Have mercy upon me, O God, according to thy lovingkindness: according unto the multitude of thy tender mer-

cies blot out my transgressions. Wash me throughly from mine iniquity, and cleanse me from my sin. For I acknowledge my transgressions: and my sin is ever before me. Against thee, thee only, have I sinned, and done this evil in thy sight: that thou mightest be justified when thou speakest, and be clear when thou judgest. Behold, I was shapen in iniquity; and in sin did my mother conceive me (Psalm 51:1-5).

David's writings in the Psalms are as revealing as his reign. Nearly half[8] of the Psalms are specifically ascribed to David, and possibly some of the anonymous Psalms were written by him as well. The Psalms are more frequently quoted in the New Testament than any other Old Testament book, and are often given as the words of David. His gifts were poetic and prophetic. Few Bible passages are better known, or have comforted more people, than David's shepherd Psalm, the twenty-third.

David, like Joseph, was severely tested in his youth, because God was preparing him to typify and remind us of that **Greater David**, our Lord and Savior Jesus Christ.

Questions for Consideration and Discussion

1. When did the spirit of the Lord come upon David?
2. Why was it necessary to keep his anointing secret?
3. What were three of David's most heroic tests?
4. What is so special about the David/Jonathan friendship?

5. Where did David go for relief from Saul's perpetual rage?
6. Was it right to feign madness or tell lies in self-defense?
7. What were some of David's greatest weaknesses?
8. What were some of his greatest strengths?
9. How was David a man after God's own heart?
10. Why did he suffer so many wars and family conflicts?

---

1. Acts 13:21
2. 2 Samuel 5:4
3. 1 Samuel 19:11, 15, 20
4. 1 Samuel 24:3-7; 26:7-12
5. Deuteronomy 17:17
6. 2 Samuel 5:13; 1 Chronicales 14:3
7. 1 Kings 2:45b; 2 Samuel 7:16; Psalm 89:3, 4; 132:11-14
8. 73 Psalms are ascribed to David

12

God Also Uses Pagan Kings

*The king's heart is in the hand of the LORD, . . .
he turneth it whithersoever he will
(Proverbs 21:1).*

God was at work not only in **saints** of old, but even in pagan kings. Some of them, as we shall see, may have thought they were in control, while the Sovereign Hand of God was only using them as a disciplinary tool to correct His own people. The fate of these kings was also in God's hand. He accomplishes His purpose even through those who do not trust Him.

I. Shalmaneser, King of Assyria

"O Assyrian, the rod of mine anger . . ."

About 722 B.C., when Israel, the Northern Kingdom, had rejected the God of their fathers too long for His marvelous patience to endure them any longer, He gave them into the hands of the king of Assyria (2 Kings 17:1-6). The Assyrians, of course, were no better than Israel, but the children of Israel had been instructed and carried as God's chosen people, and were therefore more responsible than Assyria. Shalmaneser himself did not know God, and did not realize that he was only an instrument in the hands of God, disciplining God's own people. Concerning that situation the Lord said,

> *O Assyrian, the rod of mine anger, and the staff in their hand is mine indignation. . . . Howbeit he meaneth not so, neither doth his heart think so; but it is in his heart to destroy and cut off nations not a few (Isaiah 10:5, 7).*

See Shalmaneser's haughty boasts in Isaiah 10:8-15.

II. Nebuchadnezzar, King of Babylon

"The LORD carried away Judah and Jerusalem **by the hand of Nebuchadnezzar"** *(1 Chronicles 6:15b)*

By 586 B.C. Judah, the Southern Kingdom, had likewise fallen. God gave them into the hands of Nebuchadnezzar, the king of Babylon. He totally destroyed the magnificent temple at Jerusalem, burned the city, and carried all their treasures and most of the Hebrew people to Babylon. At that time, Nebuchadnezzar basically controlled the kingdoms of the world, including Assyria. He also was ignorant of the fact that He was an instrument used of God to punish wicked nations, and that his own destruction would soon be coming. What God had said of the Assyrian, applied equally well to Nebuchadnezzar, whom He designated as *"my servant"* (Jeremiah 25:9). See especially Jeremiah 27:6-8.

God even gave Nebuchadnezzar a remarkable dream, showing him as the head of all the major world empires in their successive orders, followed by a final kingdom that shall *"stand for ever"* (Daniel 2:1-44). His sleep was gone, and all he could remember was that the dream troubled him, but he could not recall any part of the dream. His magicians, astrologers, and sorcerers insisted there was not a man upon the earth that could show him what he had dreamed.

But to Daniel, one of his enslaved Hebrew captives, God gave an accurate revelation of the dream and the interpretations thereof. Those empires have risen and fallen exactly as Daniel interpreted them, down to the last temporal one. It proves that God, and not man, was then,and still is, in control of events. Truly *"the most High ruleth in the kingdom of men, and giveth it to whomsover he will, and setteth up over it the basest of men"* (Daniel 4:17b).

Finally God gave Nebuchadnezzar another dream, forewarning him of his own humiliation, which came upon him suddenly twelve months later. When that was over, Nebuchadnezzar who for a while had ruled the world, confessed that God is in control, and that *"all the inhabitants of the earth are reputed as nothing."*[1]

Even before Jerusalem fell, God had already revealed how long their captivity would last, named their deliverer, and scheduled their restoration:

> *And this whole land* [of Judah] *shall be a desolation, and an astonishment; and these nations shall serve the king of Babylon **seventy years.** And it shall come to pass, **when seventy years are accomplished,** that I will punish the king of Babylon, and that nation, saith the* LORD, *for their iniquity, and the land of the Chaldeans, and will make it* [Babylon] *perpetual desolations (Jeremiah 25:11, 12).*

III. Cyrus, King of Persia

For the initial restoration of Israel, God first employed another Gentile monarch more honorable than Nebuchadnezzar. Cyrus at least gave recognition to God (Ezra 1:2).

> *That saith of Cyrus, He is **my shepherd,** and shall perform all my pleasure: even saying to Jerusalem, Thou shalt be built; and to the temple, Thy foundation shall be laid.*

> *Thus saith the* LORD *to **his anointed,** to Cyrus, whose right hand I have holden, to subdue nations before him; and I will loose the loins of kings, to open before him the two leaved gates; and the gates shall not be shut"* (Isaiah 44:28, 45:1).

Amazingly, Isaiah wrote this prophecy a hundred years before Cyrus was born, possibly one hundred seventy-five years before Cyrus became king. God named him Cyrus, designated him as His **shepherd,** His **anointed,** and was very specific about what Cyrus would accomplish at Jerusalem. The date for this event was added by Jeremiah shortly before Jerusalem fell.

*Now in the first year of Cyrus king of Persia, **that the word of the LORD spoken by the mouth of Jeremiah might be accomplished,** the LORD stirred up the spirit of Cyrus king of Persia, that he made a proclamation throughout all his kingdom, and put it also in writing, saying, Thus saith Cyrus king of Persia, All the kingdoms of the earth hath the LORD God of heaven given me; and he hath charged me to build him an house in Jerusalem, which is in Judah. Who is there among you of all his people? The LORD his God be with him, and let him go up (2 Chronicles 36:22, 23).*[2]

Cyrus freely encouraged the Jews to go back to Jerusalem to rebuild the city and the temple. He restored the five thousand four hundred vessels that Nebuchadnezzar had brought to Babylon, and requested others to help them with whatever they needed. Forty-nine thousand, six hundred ninety-seven Jews returned at that time, under the leadership of Zerubbabel (read Ezra 1 and 2).

But they encountered opposition from the people of the land, who hired counselors against them, frustrating their purpose all the days of Cyrus. In fact the work actually ceased until the second year of Darius (Ezra 4:24), which was fifteen or more years. So it happened precisely as Isaiah had predicted before Cyrus was born. Cyrus gave orders to build the city, and his servant Sheshbazzar laid the foundation for the temple (Ezra 5:16). The temple, however, was not finished until the sixth year of King Darius (Ezra 6:15), a later successor whom the LORD used to stop the resistance and to rebuild both the temple and the city. **God is always in control!**

Questions for Consideration and Discussion

1. What was the capital city of Assyria?
2. Through what prophet was that city once spared?
3. What wicked Hebrew kings had misled the Northern Kingdom?
4. Who was the outstanding prophet of this kingdom?
5. How much longer did the Southern Kingdom last?
6. Who were the outstanding prophets in Judah?
7. What famous prophets were captives in Babylon?
8. Did Cyrus know that God named him before his birth?
9. What made Cyrus more honorable than Nebuchadnezzar?
10. To what prophet did Persian kings give notable assignments?
11. What other Jew was given political powers by a pagan king?

---

1. Daniel 4:1-37
2. Also recorded in Ezra 1:1-3a

13

Four Jewish Slaves Resisted Peer Pressure

God gave them knowledge and skill
in all learning and wisdom
(Daniel 1:17b).

Daniel, Hananiah, Mishael, and Azariah were born at the beginning of one of the darkest periods in Hebrew history. Jehoiakim, the godless king who spitefully burned Jeremiah's writings,[1] reigned in Jerusalem, and Judah as a nation was insulting God by worshipping idols. Therefore, God gave Jerusalem into the hands of Nebuchadnezzar, a Babylonian king, to punish His own people for their sins. They besieged and finally captured Jerusalem, leading thousands of Jews captive into Babylon.

Daniel and his three friends were taken in the first of three deportations. Apparently, they were members of the royal family of Judah, probably teenagers, selected to be trained for royal service to the king of Babylon (Daniel 1:3, 4). Evidently deprived of normal manhood, they were to serve as eunuchs among the king's staff. To further emphasize their captors' dominion over them, their God-honoring Hebrew names were changed to Belteshazzar, Shadrach, Meshach, and Abednego, to honor the pagan gods of Babylon. The Chaldeans did everything possible to destroy the faith and heritage of their Jewish captives. In spite of such humiliation, these four young men served faithfully in their various assignments.

They purposed in their hearts that they would not defile themselves with the dainties and the wine prescribed by the king. Imagine the peer pressure faced by these four faithful boys, when all the other Jewish captives ate and drank like the Chaldeans. Humbly and tactfully Daniel asked for a ten-day diet and health test. Those four boys fared much better on vegetables and water than those who ate the king's royal fare and drank his wine. Therefore, their choice of diet was granted them. They were given three years of special Chaldean training, *"that at the end thereof they might stand before the king"* (Daniel 1:5).

As for these four children, **God gave them knowledge and skill** *in all learning and wisdom: and Daniel had understanding in all visions and dreams. . . . And in all matters of wisdom and understanding, that the king inquired of them, he found them ten times better than all the magicians and astrologers that were in all his realm. And Daniel continued even unto the first year of king Cyrus (Daniel 1:17, 20, 21).*

Although this was a select group with high potential, God obviously provided divine enablement far beyond their normal capacity. Daniel was given grace to interpret all visions and dreams. He served in captivity for more than seventy years, apparently to the end of his life.

Daniel Interprets Nebuchadnezzar's Dream

God had given Nebuchadnezzar a dream that troubled him, and he could not remember what he had dreamed. All his magicians, astrologers, and sorcerers said they would show him the interpretation if he would tell them the dream. The king reasoned correctly that if they could tell him what he had dreamed, then he could trust their interpretation as well. But the Chaldeans said, *"There is not a man upon the earth that can show the king's matter"* (Daniel 2:10).

That angered the king, and he decreed that all the wise men of Babylon should be slain, even Daniel and his friends. Daniel asked the king to give him a little time, and he would tell him the dream and the interpretation. He and his companions went home and prayed until the dream and its interpretation were revealed to Daniel in a vision. Then Daniel blessed God with a prayer of praise and thanksgiving that shows how thoroughly he was assured of God's answer (2:19-23).

When they brought him to the king, he did not

mention his own involvement, but said, *"There is a God in heaven that revealeth secrets, and maketh **known to the king Nebuchadnezzar what shall be in the latter days**. Thy dream, and the visions of thy head upon thy bed, are these"* (Daniel 2:28). As Daniel told the dream, the king evidently recalled and sensed the accuracy of it. By that he was assured that the interpretation is also correct (Daniel 2:27-36).

The dream was a preview of four major world empires from that day to the end of time. They were pictured in the form of a man whose head was of gold; the breast and arms of silver; the trunk and thighs of brass; the legs of iron; and feet of iron mixed with clay. Daniel interpreted the whole dream in detail, down to the last empire, of which the final phase is still in the making. He made it very plain that the God of heaven was in control, and not the gods of Babylon.

It is indeed amazing that God revealed so much eschatology to a pagan king, but it is understandable that He revealed it through one of that king's Jewish captives. God prepared Daniel to reveal these secrets not only to Nebuchadnezzar, but to you and me, and to all people everywhere, from 605 B. C. to the end of time. It's a *landmark* and a *timepiece* that He wants Christians to treat with reverence.

Three Whom They Could Not Burn
Nebuchadnezzar made an image of gold nine feet

square and ninety feet high. Then he called a mass meeting to dedicate and worship this great image of gold. They used all kinds of instrumental music to whip up enthusiasm, and demanded that everyone must worship that image. The king decreed that *"whoso falleth not down and worshippeth shall the same hour be cast into the midst of a burning fiery furnace"* *(Daniel 3:6).*

We don't know where Daniel was at the time, but his three friends, who refused to worship the idol, were summoned before the king. In his rage and fury he vigorously pronounced that either they worship or burn, then defiantly exclaimed, *"Who is that God that shall deliver you out of my hands!"* (Daniel 3:15).

> *If it be so, our God whom we serve is able to deliver us from the burning fiery furnace, and he will deliver us out of thine hand, O king. But if not, be it known unto thee, O king, that we will not serve thy gods, nor worship the golden image which thou hast set up (Daniel 3:17, 18).*

Full of fury, the king commanded that the furnace be heated seven times hotter than usual, and commanded his most mighty men to bind those three men and throw them into that overheated furnace. The fire was so hot it killed the men who threw them in, but it could not even singe a hair on the head of Shadrach, Meshach, or Abednego—nor on the Lord Jesus Christ who had joined them in the fire.

Then *Nebuchadnezzar spake, and said, Blessed*

be the God of Shadrach, Meshach, and Abednego, who hath sent his angel, and delivered his servants that trusted in him, and have changed the king's word, and yielded their bodies, that they might not serve nor worship any god, except their own God. Therefore I make a decree, That every people, nation, and language, which speak any thing amiss against the God of Shadrach, Meshach, and Abednego, shall be cut in pieces, and their houses shall be made a dunghill: because there is no other God that can deliver after this sort (Daniel 3:28, 29).

Daniel Survives International Revolutions

Daniel lived in captivity under five successive kings: three Chaldeans (Nebuchadnezzar, Evil-Merodach, and Belshazzar), Darius the Mede, and Cyrus the Persian.

Belshazzar, the last Babylonian king, made a feast for a thousand of his lords. They drank wine from the sacred vessels taken from the temple at Jerusalem, and praised the gods of gold, silver, brass, iron, wood and stone. Suddenly they saw a hand writing on the wall, but could not read the writing. Again they called for Daniel, who read the writing and interpreted the meaning:

MENE: God hath numbered they kingdom, and finished it.

TEKEL: Thou art weighed in the balances, and art found wanting.

PERES: Thy kingdom is divided, and given to the Medes and Persians.

In that night was Belshazzar the king of the Chaldeans slain. And Darius the Median took the kingdom, being about threescore and two years old (Daniel 5:30, 31).

That was a revolution—a complete takeover by another kingdom. It was the kind of thing that today would fill many pages of every daily newspaper in the country. But Daniel tells the story with twenty-five words. His King was the God of heaven, and Daniel's business went on as usual. God was still on the throne and in control!

Daniel Unharmed in the Lions' Den

Darius appointed a hundred and twenty princes to oversee his kingdom, and over them he set three presidents, of whom Daniel was first. *"Because an excellent spirit was in* [Daniel], *the king thought to set him over the whole realm."* The other presidents and princes, being jealous, conspired against Daniel. Finding no fault in him, except that he regularly prayed to God, they ensnared Darius by flattery. They induced him to *"make a firm decree, that whosover shall ask a petition of any God or man for thirty days, save of thee, O king, he shall be cast into the den of lions"* (Daniel 6:7). That, they assumed, would eliminate Daniel.

Daniel, of course, prayed and gave thanks three times a day, just as he had before. Then these men assembled and insisted that Darius comply with the decree he had signed. *"Know, O king,"* they warned, *"that the law of the Medes and Persians is, That no decree nor statute which the king establisheth may be changed"* (Daniel 6:15). They settled for nothing less. Daniel was cast into the den of lions, and a stone sealed with the king's signet was laid on the mouth of the den.

The king spent the night fasting. Early the next morning he hastened to the den and found Daniel alive and well.

> *And the king commanded, and they brought those men which had accused Daniel, and they cast* them *into the den of lions, them, their children, and their wives; and the lions had the mastery of them, and brake all their bones in pieces or ever they came at the bottom of the den. Then king Darius wrote unto all people, nations, and languages, that dwell in all the earth; Peace be multiplied unto you. I make a decree, That in every dominion of my kingdom men tremble and fear before the God of Daniel: for he is the living God, and stedfast for ever, and his kingdom* that *which shall not be destroyed, and his dominion* shall be even *unto the end (Daniel 6:24-26).*

Daniel Prays for His People

The basic purpose of this book is not interpretation of prophesy, but seeing God at work in the lives of people who trust Him, and some who don't. In Daniel we see God responding to a man of prayer. Daniel understood that Israel had sinned against God, bringing their dispersion upon themselves. He gave himself to prayer *"with fasting, and sackcloth, and ashes."* He prayed and confessed in the *first person:* **We** have sinned; neither have **we** hearkened; unto **us** belongs confusion of faces; because **we** have sinned; **we** have rebelled; **we** have done wickedly. Through the entire prayer he included himself as if he were guilty of all the sins of Israel, and fervently prayed for them all (Daniel 9:3-19).

While he was still praying, Gabriel was sent to give him skill and understanding about God's specific dealing with Israel in the future. Not only would their captivity in Babylon last seventy years, but he mapped out for them **seventy weeks (sevens) of years** divided into three separate and distinct periods of time. Not during, but *"after threescore and two weeks shall Messiah be cut off"* (Daniel 9:26).

Daniel, Paul, and John all got their messages from the same Infallible Source. Their messages support and complement each other, and all three give vital information about end-time events. Some of it is beyond the grasp of our limited comprehension, and we have varied interpretations of how it will be. Rather than quarrel about our views, we commit our differences to Him who designed it all.

Questions for Consideration and Discussion

1. What kind of boys had the king told his men to bring?

2. What effect was intended by changing their names?

3. What was wrong about the king's meat and drink?

4. How do you explain the boys' superior intelligence?

5. Why did God give those dreams to Nebuchadnezzar?

6. What did the other Jews do about the golden image?

7. Couldn't they just bow and worship God, not the image?

8. How was Daniel affected by the national turnovers?

9. Under how many kings and kingdoms did he serve?

10. How did Daniel spend the night in the lion's den?

---

1. Jeremiah 36:23

14

Two Reformers in Postexilic Israel

I. A Man Who Honored God's Word

For Ezra had prepared his heart to seek the law of the LORD, **and to do** *it, and to teach in Israel statutes and judgments (Ezra 7:10).*

Ezra, a Levite, and a descendant of Aaron (Ezra 7:1-6), was born and reared in Babylon, but instructed in the Jewish faith as *"a ready scribe in the law of Moses."* He was brilliant, well educated, and thoroughly dedicated to the Word of God and the work of the Lord. He made a record by families of the Jews who, at the decree of Cyrus, king of Persia, had gone to Jerusalem with Zerubbabel: a grand total of forty-nine thousand, six hundred ninety-seven (Ezra 2:2-65).

Eighty years later, in the seventh year of Artaxerxes, king of Persia, Ezra led a group of 1,754 males back to Jerusalem, (Ezra 8:2-20), bringing the combined total to fifty-one thousand four hundred fifty-one returnees recorded by that time.

Ezra had letters from Artaxerxes to all the treasurers beyond the river, commanding that whatsoever Ezra required should be done speedily. He was authorized to appoint judges and magistrates and to execute severe discipline upon any who violated the law of God or of the king.

Ezra was shocked when he learned how the Jews who had returned earlier had taken strange wives of the people of the land, which God had expressly forbidden. See how he mourned, fasted, prayed, and toiled, sparing no pains to bring them to repentance.

> *And when I heard this thing, I rent my garment and my mantle, and plucked off the hair of my head and of my beard, and sat down astonied (Ezra 9:3).*

> *And at the evening sacrifice . . . I fell upon my knees, and spread out my hands unto the LORD my God, And said, O my God, I am ashamed and blush to lift up my face to thee, my God: for our iniquities are increased over our head, and our trespass is grown up unto the heavens. Since the days of our fathers have we been in a great trespass unto this day; and for our iniquities have we, our kings, and our priests, been delivered into the hand of the kings of the lands, to the sword, to captivity, and to a spoil, and to confusion of face, as it is this day (Ezra 9:5-7).*

For six more verses his prayer continued. He ate no bread and drank no water, *"for he mourned because of the transgression of them that had been carried away"* (Ezra 10:6). The people rallied behind Ezra and agreed to do whatever the Lord required. Ezra said further,

> *Now therefore make confession unto the* Lord *God of your fathers, and do his pleasure: and separate your-selves from the people of the land, and from the strange wives (Ezra 10:11).*

The situation was handled in an orderly fashion, in cooperation with their judges, city by city and family by family. In three months the task was completed. One hundred thirteen men had taken strange wives, which apparently were all put away, so that the fierce wrath of our God would be turned away. According to the original language in Ezra 10:15, there were only four men who opposed this procedure.

This separation is not an endorsement of divorce, but a return to God's basic instructions given before the children of Israel entered Canaan. God had instructed them to utterly destroy those idol-worship-ping nations, lest they lead Israel astray. They were strictly forbidden to intermarry with them.

> *Neither shalt thou make marriages with them; thy daughter thou shalt not give unto his son, nor his daughter shalt thou take unto thy son.* **For they will turn away thy son from following me,** *that they may serve other gods: so will the anger of the* Lord *be kindled against you, and destroy thee suddenly (Deu-teronomy 7:3, 4).*

Because of their intermingling with those nations

that led Israel into idolatry, God had given them into the Babylonian captivity. Now they were doing it again, directly contrary to God's revealed will. God sent Ezra to their rescue, to restore order and to teach them respect for God's law. Ezra successfully completed his assignment.

II. Nehemiah, the Organizer and Reformer

Then contended I with the rulers, and said, Why is the house of God forsaken? And I gathered them together, and set them in their place (Nehemiah 13:11).

The name Nehemiah first occurs in Ezra 2:2, as one who returned with Zerubbabel. The same man is also listed in Nehemiah 7:7 as one of that number, and that is all we find of him. That occurred during the first year of Cyrus, before the younger Nehemiah of our present study was born.

Nehemiah, the son of Hachaliah, came to Jerusalem about ninety years later, in the twentieth year of Artaxerxes King of Persia (Nehemiah 2:1). Having inquired about the situation at Jerusalem of certain Jews who returned from there, he was deeply grieved about the deplorable conditions of the city. He yearned to go to Jerusalem to help in its restoration. Notice how he fasted and earnestly prayed, including himself as guilty of their national sins (Nehemiah 1:4-11).

Nehemiah had a high position in the palace as the king's cupbearer. But why was he *"very sore afraid"*[1] when the king asked why he looked so sad? It seemed like a fearful risk to ask for a leave, until the king rather unexpectedly asked what he desired. That gave a ray of hope, but he did some earnest praying, and then proceeded very cautiously. He needed to obtain permission, and to set a length of time for his leave. As a servant of the king, he was certainly not his own boss.

He did, however, obtain the permission he sought when the king was in one of his better moods. The king must have been favorably affected by the queen sitting by him (Nehemiah 2:6). He granted a limited leave, possibly long enough to build the wall, and even commissioned Nehemiah to operate in the King's name with royal authority.

Nehemiah came to Jerusalem and spent about three days and nights evaluating the situation. He prayed and planned before exposing his intentions to anyone. The abundance of rubbish everywhere was a most discouraging factor. With that challenge before him, Nehemiah, the Organizer and Encourager, swung into action and did a tremendous work. He firmly announced, *"The God of heaven, he will prosper us; therefore we his servants will arise and build."* His enthusiasm motivated everyone, giving them a mind to work.

In addition to building the wall, he had to deal with other serious problems. The rich among their own people were taking advantage of the poor, even taking their mortgaged lands, vineyards, and oliveyards. Some of the poorest had already given of their children into slavery, and had no means to redeem them (Nehemiah 5:5). Nehemiah rebuked the oppressors, convincing them to quit charging interest on money they loaned to the poor, and to restore whatever land they had taken.

Their most difficult problem was the interference and attacks of outside enemies. Sanballat the Horonite, Tobiah the Ammonite, and Geshem the Arabian were very angry, and conspired together to fight against Jerusalem, and to hinder the rebuilding (Nehemiah 4:8). Nehemiah armed his workers with swords and spears. His slogan was, *"Be not ye afraid of them: remember the Lord, which is great and terrible, and fight for your brethren, . . . our God will fight for us"* (Nehemiah 4:14b, 20b). Thus, with enemies all around and the grace of God upon them, in fifty-two days they finished the wall (Nehemiah 6:15).

When the wall was finished, it appears as though the allotted time of Nehemiah's temporary leave may have been up. He appointed others to take charge in his absence (Nehemiah 7:1-3). Some think he went back to Babylon and obtained an extension to his commission. He was soon back on the job, for we see the Tirshatha (governor) was functioning again,[2] and *"Nehemiah . . . is the Tirshatha,"* a position he held for twelve years (Nehemiah 8:9; 10:1).

The Ezra-Nehemiah Team

In those days there was no printing press. Every single copy of the Mosaic law had to be laborously copied by hand. Since sin and mistakes had the same birthday, mistakes did slip into some hand-copied manuscripts. (How many hours can you copy error free by hand?) Ezra the scribe collected and compared copies of the Pentateuch, the Psalms, and the Prophets in a diligent effort to make new copies as error free as man could produce. Many of these people had never seen a written copy of the Scriptures, nor heard a reading thereof.

Then the people gathered together into the street to hear Ezra read the law. On the first day of the seventh month, the Jewish New Year, he read from morning till noon (Nehemiah 8:1-3). Later, he stood on a pulpit of wood made for the purpose, with thirteen men who stood with him, and when he opened the Book, all the people stood up. Ezra and his helpers read distinctly, explained the meaning, and caused the people to understand. When they heard the law, and realized how amiss their lives had been, all the people wept.

They kept the Feast of Tabernacles for seven days, from the fifteenth day of Tishri through the twenty-first, climaxed by a holy sabbath the next day (Leviticus 23:33-44). These people had not seen such a hearty feast in all their life. They had a revival! Ezra was the scribe and teacher, and Nehemiah the Tirshatha.

Now in the twenty and fourth day of this month
the children of Israel were assembled with fasting, and
with sackclothes, and earth upon them. And the seed
of Israel separated themselves from all strangers, and
stood and confessed their sins, and the iniquities of
their fathers. And they stood up in their place, and
read in the book of the law of the LORD *their God one*
fourth part of the day; and another *fourth part they*
confessed, and worshipped the LORD *their God (Nehe-*
miah 9:1-3).

Nehemiah came to Jerusalem in the twentieth year
of Artaxerxes and was there twelve years, keeping
order and directing affairs in both the church and
state. When his commission expired, he returned to
Babylon. After some time he again got permission
from the king to go back and check on things at
Jerusalem, and found plenty to do.

Tobiah the Ammonite had moved into the temple
where the meat offerings and supplies for the Levites
had been stored. The Levites were not receiving their
tithes; merchants were violating the sabbath; and the
Jews were again marrying strange wives. A grand-
son of the high priest was a son-in-law to Sanballat
the Horonite. Nehemiah 13 describes this house-
cleaning session.

Ezra and Nehemiah, working together as a team,
were shining examples of God at work in sanctified
vessels of clay. Their enthusiasm was catching, and
their diligence was most rewarding, as willing workers in the hand of God.

Questions for Consideration and Discussion

1. Where did Ezra and Nehemiah get their education?
2. From which tribe of Israel did Ezra descend?
3. How long after Zerubbabel went, did Ezra go to Jerusalem?
4. How many Jews had already married strange wives?
5. What are some causes of instability among Jewish captives?
6. What did Ezra do to get them better informed?
7. What was Nehemiah's occupation in Babylon?
8. Were either of these two men married?
9. How long after Zerubbabel went, did Nehemiah go up?
10. What was Nehemiah's main business at Jerusalem?

---

1. Nehemiah 2:2
2. Nehemiah 7:65, 70

15

From a Maiden of Faith to a Mother of Fame

In a Village of Questionable Reputation

"*Can there any good thing come out of Nazareth?*" Thus questioned mild-natured Nathanael, "*an Israelite indeed, in whom is no guile*" (John 1:46, 48). It was a dspised little village in the land of Galilee, a country frowned upon by the Pharisees as incapable of producing a prophet (John 7:52). They too were mistaken: for Jonah and Nahum both came out of Galilee.

Neither the size nor the reputation of the village could hamper the development of marvelous faith in the pure heart of a humble peasant maid. The Bible is silent about her family and her life until after her engagement to a godly man named Joseph. Her mother's name is not revealed, and her father's name appears only once in the Scripture.

The maiden's name and character, however, were both known and highly favored in heaven. The angel Gabriel was sent to her from God with the message for which God's people had waited some four thousand years.

And the angel said unto her, Fear not, Mary: for thou hast found favour with God. And, behold, thou shalt conceive in thy womb, and bring forth a son, and shalt call his name JESUS. He shall be great, and shall be called the Son of the Highest: and the Lord God shall give unto him the throne of his father David: And he shall reign over the house of Jacob for ever; and of his kingdom there shall be no end (Luke 1:30-33).

Mary's Marvelous Faith

Mary's faith surpassed that of Zacharias the priest. Surely Zacharias knew of Sarai, who had been barren until she was ninety years old, and then gave birth to Isaac, and of others like Rebekah, Rachel, and Hannah, who had been barren for a long time before giving birth. These were all cases of activating normal physical processes that had failed before. Yet when the angel told him, *"Thy wife Elizabeth shall bear thee a son,"* he asked, *"Whereby shall I know this?"* Was it not enough that the angel told him so?[1]

Mary, however, was a virgin! This birth was to be a miracle that transcended all natural laws of reproduction. It was something that had never happened before! Yet Mary never questioned the truth of what the angel said, but simply asked for more information: *"How shall this be, seeing I know not a man?"* When the angel explained, she calmly and submissively said, *"Behold the handmaid of the Lord; be it unto me according to thy word."* As if to say, "Lord, I'm not sure that I understand it all, but I trust You. I am giving myself to You, to do with me whatever You choose."[2]

The Virgin Birth was a Wonder of Wonders, an absolute essential for our salvation, and especially designed by God Almighty. God, through the Holy Spirit prepared, in a virgin womb, a body for Jesus Christ with undefiled human flesh, and equipped Him with **moral blood** totally free from any effects of sin. Since the fall of man, there has been no other truly moral blood on this earth.

Mary Visits Elizabeth

The angel also told Mary that her cousin Elizabeth, Zacharias' wife, who was known as a barren woman, was now in the sixth month of pregnancy. Now that she herself was entering a similar situation, Mary wanted some sharing time with her older cousin. She hastened to the home of Elizabeth, some sixty miles south of Nazareth, and stayed with her for three months. Study carefully Elizabeth's welcome and Mary's salutation in Luke 1:41-55.

We must, however, call attention to one thing Mary expressed in what is known as the Magnificat. *"My soul doth magnify the Lord, and my spirit hath rejoiced in **God my Saviour**."* Mary acknowledged herself as a sinner in **need of a Saviour**, just like all the rest of us. Neither she nor God ever approved of the idea that Mary should be worshipped. She was a holy woman, but not a sinless one.

Mary's Moral Purity

Mary, in contrast to Tamar, Rahab, and Bathsheba, was morally pure and undefiled. When Joseph, the godly man to whom she was espoused, learned that Mary was with child, he was shocked. But because he loved her too much to expose her openly, he planned to put her away secretly. That reveals the purity of Joseph's mind and character, which God knew firsthand. God came quickly to Joseph's rescue, and assured him of Mary's purity.

> *But while he thought on these things, behold, the angel of the Lord appeared unto him in a dream, saying, Joseph, thou son of David, fear not to take unto thee Mary thy wife: for that which is conceived in her is of the Holy Ghost. And she shall bring forth a son, and thou shalt call his name JESUS: for he shall save his people from their sins (Matthew 1:20, 21).*
>
> *Then Joseph being raised from sleep did as the angel of the Lord had bidden him, and took unto him his wife: And knew her not till she had brought forth her firstborn son: and he called his name JESUS (Matthew 1:24, 25).*

Mary's Threefold Loyalty

Mary was loyal to God as a willing servant, to Joseph as a faithful wife, and to Jesus as a loving mother. For her it was an inconvenient time to make the trip by donkey from Nazareth to Bethlehem, but she did it willingly for Joseph's sake. After Jesus was born, they were instructed by an angel to flee to Egypt, *"For Herod will seek the young child to destroy him"* (Matthew 2:13b). Again she complied willingly, this time for Jesus' sake, whose life was threatened. When an angel informed them that Herod was dead, they returned to their home in Nazareth.

At the eligible age of twelve, Jesus accompanied His parents to the eight-day Passover feast at Jerusalem. It was His first opportunity to personally interview the top doctors of the Jewish law, and He made full use of it. On the morning after the feast, while all the Jews from Nazareth started their homeward trek together, Jesus went about His Father's business and began His interviews with top officials at the Jerusalem headquarters.

All day long Joseph and Mary were confident that Jesus was somewhere among that caravan of people homeward bound. They knew Him as never being delinquent, but were not aware that His heavenly Father had special business for Him that day in Jerusalem. In the evening they investigated, and Jesus was not to be found among them. Only faintly can we visualize the anxiety they experienced—however, perhaps somewhat modified by their knowledge of who Jesus really was.

Back in Jerusalem *"they found him in the temple, sitting in the midst of the doctors, both hearing them and asking them questions. And all that heard him were astonished at his understanding and answers"* (Luke 2:46, 47).

Jesus had been so completely absorbed with His interviews that He seemed to be surprised that they sought him sorrowing. He asked, *"How is it that ye sought me? wist ye not that I must be about my Father's business"* (Luke 2:49). Although they could not fully understand His response, they seemed to sense that all was well.

Jesus went home with them, *"and was subject unto them: **but his mother kept all these sayings in her heart.** And Jesus increased in wisdom and stature, and in favor with God and man"* (Luke 2:51b, 52). Those few words briefly summarize the next eighteen years of Jesus' and Mary's lives.

Mary as a Busy Mother

In spite of the widely-spread teachings that Mary had no other children, it is quite evident in the Scriptures that she gave birth to and mothered four other sons and at least two daughters.

> *Is not this the carpenter's son? is not his mother called Mary? and his brethren, James, and Joses, and Simon, and Judas? And his sisters, are they not all with us? Whence then hath this man all these things?* (Matthew 13:55, 56).

You may ask, "Why, then, did His brothers not believe in Him?" Can you imagine the contrast between the perfect Son of God as a teenager and His unconverted half-brothers? Jesus at twelve years of age amazed the rabbinical doctors with His understanding. Even Mary, who probably understood Jesus better than anyone else, could not fully understand the difference between her unconverted sons and Jesus. But when Jesus rose from the dead, His brothers' eyes were opened, and they believed in Him. His brother James later became bishop of the church at Jerusalem, and Judas wrote the Epistle of Jude.

Mary During Jesus' Ministry

The Bible makes no mention of Joseph after that Passover feast at Jerusalem. It is generally assumed that Mary was a widow before Jesus began His ministry. Mary is mentioned again for the first time at the wedding in Cana. Jesus and His disciples also attended. Mary seemingly had some official duties there. At least when there was a shortage of wine she reported it to Jesus, obviously expecting Him to provide a solution. He responded that His hour was not yet come. Still confident that He would provide, she simply told the servants, *"Whatsoever he saith unto you, do it"* (John 2:2-5). Obviously, she fully trusted Him.

Mary at the Cross of Jesus

Now there stood by the cross of Jesus his mother, and his mother's sister, Mary the wife of Cleophas, and Mary Magdalene (John 19:25).

This was now some thirty-three years since the virgin birth, and the pain she suffered at Calvary far exceeded the birth pains she had in Bethlehem. This was the sword piercing through her own soul, as predicted by Simeon (Luke 2:35).

John, the disciple whom Jesus loved, was also standing by, probably close by Mary. Jesus, as her firstborn Son, in His dying hours provided for His widowed mother's future by committing her to John's care. And from that hour John took her unto his own home (John 19:26, 27). John, *"the disciple whom Jesus loved,"* seemed closer to the heart of Jesus than a physical brother. No one was better qualified to care for the widowed mother of our Lord than John, the disciple whom Jesus loved.

The Biblical record of Mary's life ends at a ten-day prayer meeting in the upper room (Acts 1:13, 14), but her fame continues to circle the earth, with millions of namesakes in hundreds of countries. No other name is found so often. According to Elsden C. Smith, quoted by Herbert Lockyer in *All the Women of the Bible,* it was estimated more than ten years ago that America alone had 3,720,000 women named Mary. Then we have its derivatives, such as Marie, Marion, and Marian, which would add another million plus. In the fullest sense of the word, the Mother of Jesus has risen from a lowly maiden of faith to a **Mother of Fame!**

Questions for Consideration and Discussion

1. What was Mary's social status and economic

level?

2. What did she have that was more vital than status?

3. What is the proof that Joseph was also a poor man?

4. Why did God select them to foster His only Son?

5. Why was the virgin birth an absolute imperative?

6. How was it different from the birth of Isaac?

7. Was marriage less important for her than virginity?

8. Why was Joseph "minded to put her away privily"?

9. What other option was there for an *unfaithful* spouse?

10. Why did Jesus select John to care for His widowed mother?

---

1. Luke 1:13, 18
2. Luke 1:35, 38

16

A Reed Transformed Into a Rock

But I have prayed for thee, that thy faith fail not: and when thou art converted, strengthen thy brethren (Luke 22:32).

A Wavering Reed

Reeds are a variety of grasses with hollow stems. They grow profusely and tall in shallow waters, usually in large clusters. Seldom, if ever, does one reed stand alone. Together they stand better. Peter was like a reed, a rugged man, but not strong enough to stand alone.

When Jesus first met Peter, He said, *"Thou art Simon the son of Jona: thou shalt be called Cephas, which is by interpretation, A stone"* (John 1:42). Peter was not the Bed Rock **(Christ Jesus)** upon which the church was to be built, but he became one of the foremost apostolic foundation stones in church building. His name appears one hundred fifty-eight times in the New Testament. Peter, James, and John became an inner-circle trio in the service of Christ.[1]

Peter was very human, unlearned but teachable, impulsive by nature, and sometimes presumptuous . He confessed that Jesus had words of eternal life, yet dared to refute His predictions about Peter. He fervently confessed Christ as the Messiah, yet cowardly denied Him three times—once with an oath.

When the rooster crowed, Peter came to his senses. He remembered what Jesus had said, *"And he went out, and wept bitterly"* (Matthew 26:69-75). He was heartbroken! We have no record of him from that point until after Jesus was risen again. Pondering what he probably suffered in those three days, I sometimes weep for him myself.

The Transforming Process

Peter's deep repentance triggered a turning point in his life. For three days he grieved, yearning intensely for an opportunity to make things right with Jesus—but Jesus had died and was buried.

Resurrection morning brought new hope. Jesus apparently had a private meeting with Peter that day. That evening the disciples were heard saying, *"The Lord is risen indeed, and hath appeared to Simon"* (Luke 24:34). Paul also wrote that the resurrected Jesus *"was seen of Cephas, then of the twelve"* (1 Corinthians 15:5). Those two statements are all that we are told of that meeting. Perhaps it was too sacred for open disclosure, but it certainly had cleansing and healing effects upon Peter.

Jesus later provided an opportunity for Peter to clear his record in the presence of witnesses, by a threefold confession of his love for Jesus. At the same time, He gave him a threefold commission to feed the Lord's lambs and sheep (John 21:15-17).

Jesus perfectly understood Peter's weaknesses; that is why He prayed for him that his faith fail not. He was also aware of Peter's strengths; that is why He surnamed him Cephas (John 1:42), asked him to strengthen his brethren, and used him mightily in spreading the gospel. Peter spent the rest of his life feeding the Lord's flock and winning converts among the Jews, the Samaritans, and the Gentiles far and wide.

We assume that Peter witnessed the ascension of Jesus from Mount Olivet. His name heads the list of those assembled in the upper room for a ten-day prayer meeting (Acts 1;13). Again, we can only surmise the mutual confessing, forgiving, and reconciling that took place in that room between brethren that once had been at strife about who was greatest among them. Cleansing from wrong attitudes is a vital part of preparing for an outpouring of the Holy Spirit.

I think it was God who moved Peter to suggest ordaining a replacement for Judas among the Twelve Apostles (Acts 1:15-26). There is no hint in the Scriptures that this was an unwarranted, presumptuous act, as some have suggested. The Holy Spirit was not delayed thereby, but was poured out upon them right on schedule. There is abundant evidence that the Holy Spirit had taken over in the life of Peter.

Solid as a Rock

At Pentecost and thereafter, Peter's preaching and doctrine were solid as a rock.

> *Ye men of Israel, hear these words; Jesus of Nazareth, a man approved of God among you by miracles and wonders and signs, which God did by him in the midst of you, as ye yourselves also know: Him, being delivered by the determinate counsel and foreknowledge of God, ye have taken, and by wicked hands have crucified and slain: Whom God hath raised up, having loosed the pains of death: because it was not possible that he should be holden of it (Acts 2:22-24).*

> *This Jesus hath God raised up, whereof we all are witnesses. Therefore being by the right hand of God exalted, and having received of the Father the promise of the Holy Ghost, he hath shed forth this, which ye now see and hear. For David is not ascended into the heavens: but he saith himself, The Lord said unto my Lord, Sit thou on my right hand, Until I make thy foes thy footstool. Therefore let all the house of Israel know assuredly, that God hath made that same Jesus, whom ye have crucified, both Lord and Christ (Acts 2:32-36).*

In Acts 3 the Lord used Peter and John to completely heal a forty year old man who had been lame from birth. That man had never walked. Suddenly he started walking and leaping and praising God. Excited crowds marveled at what these men had done. Peter very forcefully explained that this man was healed through Jesus Christ whom they had condemned and crucified, and that therefore they should repent and be converted that their sins may be blotted out.

When Peter exposed the false pretense of Ananias and Sapphira, they dropped dead. *"And great fear came upon all the church, and upon as many as heard these things"* (Acts 5:1-11). People in great numbers rushed about bringing the sick, *"that at least the shadow of Peter passing by might overshadow some of them . . . and they were healed every one"* (Acts 5:12-16).

The high priest and Sadducees, filled with indignation, imprisoned Peter and John. That night the angel of the Lord opened the prison doors and brought them out. The next morning the high priest and the senate sent their officers to bring them before the council. They found the prison locked, the keepers guarding the doors, but Peter and John were in the temple teaching the people. The captain brought them to the council, gently, for they feared the people (Acts 5:17-29). They did, however, beat them before they released them (Acts 5:40-42).

Later, the apostles at Jerusalem sent Peter and John to Samaria to undergird the work Philip had begun there. When Peter and John laid their hands on them and prayed, the Samaritans received the Holy Spirit (Acts 8:15-17). From Samaria, Peter came to Lydda, where he healed a man who had been paralyzed for eight years (Acts 9:32-35). At Joppa he raised Dorcas back to life (Acts 9:36-42).

Next, the Lord definitely used Peter to open the door of the Gospel to the Gentiles. Cornelius was a centurion of what was known as the Italian Band (all Gentile, Roman soldiers). He was a devout man who feared God with all his house and prayed to God always (Acts 10:2). In a dream, the Lord told Cornelius to *"send men to Joppa, and call for one Simon, whose surname is Peter: . . . he shall tell thee what thou oughtest to do."*

While the men from Cornelius were approaching Joppa, God used visions from heaven to prepare Peter for the request coming from a Roman centurion (Acts 10:9-16).

> *While Peter thought on the vision, the Spirit said unto him, Behold, three men seek thee. Arise therefore, and get thee down, and go with them, doubting nothing: for I have sent them (Acts 10:19, 20).*

The message was clear, and when the men told him what Cornelius had seen and heard, Peter was convinced. He took the men in and kept them overnight. The next morning, he and six other brethren went with those men, arriving at Ceasarea about mid-afternoon the following day. Cornelius and many of his friends were awaiting Peter's arrival, ready to hear his message. Peter was God's chosen vessel for this unprecedented assignment.

Thus Jesus' commission to Peter was carried out, when He said, *"I will give unto thee the keys of the kingdom of heaven: and whatsoever thou shalt bind on earth shall be bound in heaven: and whatsoever thou shalt loose on earth shall be loosed in heaven"* (Matthew 16:19). God used Peter to open Gospel doors: first, for the Jews at Pentecost; second, for the Samaritans; and third, for the Gentiles at the home of Cornelius.

When Peter came back to Jerusalem, the Jews challenged him for having eaten with uncircumcised men. He explained to them in detail the vision he had seen, the voice that had spoken to him, what the angel had said to Cornelius, and how the Holy Spirit had fallen on them as well as on the Jews.

> *Forasmuch then as God gave them the like gift as he did unto us, who believed on the Lord Jesus Christ; what was I, that I could withstand God? When they heard these things, they held their peace, and glorified God, saying, Then hath God also to the Gentiles granted repentance unto life (Acts 11:17, 18).*

It took an authority figure like Peter to convince the Jews that Christ removes *"the middle wall of partition"* (Ephesians 2:14) between Jews and Gentiles as well as between Jews and Samaritans.

About that time, Herod killed James the brother of John. When he saw that it pleased the Jews, he took Peter also. But Easter being at hand, he put Peter in prison, intending to bring him to trial after Easter. The night before his scheduled trial, Peter slept (*yes, he actually slept!*) between two soldiers, and at least two keepers guarded the prison doors (Acts 12:1-6).

However, God still had work for Peter. That night the angel of the Lord came to Peter, woke him up, and said, *"Rise up quickly."* His chains fell off his hands, and the angel led him out through the first and second wards. When they came to the iron gate, it swung open and they walked right on out. The angel took him one street further, and left him (Acts 12:7-10).

When Peter realized that his deliverance was an actual experience rather than a vision, he went to the house of Mary, the mother of John Mark, where many people were in earnest prayer for his deliverance. After telling them how God had delivered him, he departed, and went into another place (Acts 12:11-17).

Next we find Peter at the Jerusalem conference using his experience and influence to change the minds of those who had insisted that the Gentiles could not be saved unless they were circumcised.

> *And when there had been much disputing, Peter rose up, and said unto them, Men and brethren, ye know how that a good while ago God made choice among us, that the Gentiles by my mouth should hear the word of the gospel, and believe. And God, which knoweth the hearts, bare them witness, giving them*

the Holy Ghost, even as he did unto us; And put no difference between us and them, purifying their hearts by faith. Now therefore why tempt ye God, to put a yoke upon the neck of the disciples, which neither our fathers nor we were able to bear? But we believe that through the grace of the Lord Jesus Christ we shall be saved, even as they. Then all the multitude kept silence and gave audience to Barnabas and Paul" (Acts 15:7-12a).

I am not sure whether it was before or after the above conference that Peter failed a test at Antioch which he had passed very well at the house of Cornelius in Ceasarea. At Antioch, Peter had been eating with Gentiles. When certain Jews from Jerusalem came on the scene, he withdrew from the Gentiles, *"fearing them which were of the circumcision"* (Galatians 2:11-19). Paul *"withstood him to the face"* and reprimanded him. In the Galatian letter we are not told how Peter responded to the rebuke, but we do have beautiful evidence in Peter's epistle of a very gracious response.

*And account that the longsuffering of our Lord is salvation; even as **our beloved brother Paul** also according to **the wisdom given unto him** hath written unto you; as also in all his epistles, speaking in them of these things; in which are some things hard to be understood, which they that are unlearned and unstable wrest, as they do also **the other scriptures**, unto their own destruction (2 Peter 3:15, 16).*

Peter lovingly commended Paul for the wisdom given unto him, and spoke well of **all his epistles** (which includes the Galatian letter) as authentic scriptures. It shows that Peter highly respected and appreciated Paul, holding no ill feelings of any sort.

Peter was a diamond in the rough, used effectively by the mighty hand of God. Once he had been labeled as *"unlearned and ignorant,"* but led by the Holy Spirit, he wrote two epistles as dynamic and powerful as his preaching. For quality samples of Peter's writing, I quote three verses from each of his two epistles:

> *For what glory is it, if, when ye be buffeted for your faults, ye shall take it patiently? but if, when ye do well, and suffer for it, ye take it patiently, this is acceptable with God. For even hereunto were ye called: because Christ also suffered for us, leaving us an example, that ye should follow his steps (1 Peter 2:20, 21).*

> *Who his own self bare our sins in his own body on the tree, that we, being dead to sins, should live unto righteousness: by whose stripes ye were healed (1 Peter 2:24).*

> *But the day of the Lord will come as a thief in the night; in the which the heavens shall pass away with a great noise, and the elements shall melt with fervent heat, the earth also and the works that are therein shall be burned up. Seeing then that all these things shall be dissolved, what manner of persons ought ye to be in all holy conversation and godliness, Looking*

for and hasting unto the coming of the day of God,
wherein the heavens being on fire shall be dissolved,
and the elements shall melt with fervent heat? (2 Peter
3:10-12).

From the record in the *Martyrs Mirror* we learn that ultimately Peter gave his life for the cause of Christ by crucifixion at Jerusalem. Feeling unworthy to die in the same manner as Jesus, he requested to be crucified head downward. His name will be inscribed upon the foundation wall of the New Jerusalem as one of the Twelve Apostles (Revelation 21:14).

Questions for Consideration and Discussion

1. What was Peter's first introduction to Jesus?
2. What was Jesus' first comment about Peter?
3. What were Peter's most apparent strengths?
4. What were his most apparent weaknesses?
5. What virtues counterbalanced his impulsiveness?
6. What was significant about Peter's *great confession*?
7. Why did Jesus meet him privately on Resurrection Day?
8. What three doors did he open with the key Jesus gave him?
9. What incident burst the balloon of his zeal at Jesus' arrest?
10. What are the evidences that Peter was not afraid to die?

1. Mark 5:37; 9:2; Matthew 26:37

2. Background Scriptures: Matthew 14:28; 17:4; Mark 9:5; John 21:7; Matthew 16:22; John 13:8, 9; 18:10; Matthew 26:31-35; Matthew 16:16; Mark 8:29; John 6:69; Matthew 26:69-75

17

A Mad Man Reborn to Be an Apostle

Being exceedingly mad against them,
I persecuted them even unto strange cities
(Acts 26:11b).

Saul the Persecutor

Paul himself says, *"Whatsoever things were written aforetime were written for our learning"* (Romans 15:4). Therefore, as we study Paul's life together, let us be open to **God's message for us.** God's dealings with Paul are recorded for **our admonition, correction, and instruction.**

God wanted a man to bridge the chasm between Jews and Gentiles, and to proclaim Christ effectively to both. He chose a *"fireball"* by the name of Saul, whom He had to transform to make him usable. In his zeal for the law and his hatred for Christianity, he outdid his peers. His attitude and goal are best described in his own words.

> *I verily thought with myself, that I ought to do*
> *many things contrary to the name of Jesus of Naza-*

reth. Which thing I also did in Jerusalem: and many of the saints did I shut up in prison, having received authority from the chief priests; and when they were put to death, I gave my voice against them. And I punished them oft in every synagogue, and compelled them to blaspheme; and being exceedingly mad against them, I persecuted them even unto strange cities (Acts 26:9-11).

When the first Christian martyr, Stephen, was stoned to death, Saul was there giving his approval (Acts 7:58b; 22:20). Furthermore, *"he made havock of the church, entering into every house, and haling men and women, committed them to prison"* (Acts 8:3). His goal was to destroy the Christian church, and that is Satan's goal to this day.

Saul was on his way to Damascus in search of Christian believers, whom he planned to bring bound to Jerusalem for punishment or death. Suddenly, a blinding light, brighter than the noonday sun, flashed from heaven. An audible voice said, *"Saul, Saul, Why do you persecute Me? I am Jesus whom you are persecuting."*

Frightened and trembling, Saul asked sincerely, *"Lord, what do You want me to do?"* The Lord could have told him directly, but He chose to instruct Saul through one of those Christians whom Saul had hoped to bring bound to Jerusalem. **In fact, the Lord is always seeking human hands and lips to bring sinners into the fold.** He sent Ananias of Damascus to further instruct this notorious persecutor.

Ananias went, and laying his hands on Saul, said, *"Brother Saul, the Lord Jesus, who appeared to you as you came, has sent me, that you may receive your sight, and be filled with the Holy Ghost."* Immediately the scales fell from his eyes and he could see again. Saul believed, arose, and was baptized.[1]

Saul Is Reborn and Becomes an Apostle

For I speak to you Gentiles, inasmuch as I am the apostle of the Gentiles, I magnify mine office (Romans 11:13).

Saul had left Jerusalem with written authority from the chief priests to go all the way to Damascus, round up believers in Christ and bring them bound to Jerusalem. Near Damascus, he was apprehended from heaven by Jesus Himself, and commissioned instead to round up unbelievers and bring them to Christ.

From that day forward, God did many mighty works in and through Saul. Not only was his physical sight restored, but Saul was given **new insights**. He discovered that the Christ, whom he had been persecuting, is **the one and only way to eternal life**. That is an imperative lesson for you and me! It is the Truth we are to share with others.

"Then was Saul certain days with the disciples which were at Damascus. And straightway he preached Christ in the synagogues, that he was the Son of God" (Acts 9:19b, 20).

What a marvelous transformation: a raving antagonist transformed into a dynamic apostle, a wondrous work of God in an earthen vessel! Synagogues were still denouncing Christians, but immediately Saul boldly preached Christ, even in the synagogues.

Unbelieving Jews, however, plotted to kill Saul. They watched the city gates day and night. *"Then the disciples took him by night, and let him down by the wall in a basket"* (Acts 9:25). We learn from Galatians 1:17-19 that Saul then went to Arabia: undoubtedly to be emptied of self and to be filled with the Holy Spirit in **private communion with God.** Three years later he came to Jerusalem to visit Peter. As Saul then tried to testify publicly for Jesus in Jerusalem, he discovered that the traps he had helped to set three years earlier now remained set for him.

Luke added the following information about Paul's experience at Jerusalem

> *And when Saul was come to Jerusalem, he assayed to join himself to the disciples: but they were all afraid of him, and believed not that he was a disciple. But Barnabas took him, and brought him to the apostles, and declared unto them how he had seen the Lord in the way, and that he had spoken to him, and how he had preached boldly at Damascus in the name of Jesus. And he was with them coming in and going out at Jerusalem. And he spake boldly in the name of the Lord Jesus, and disputed against the Grecians: but they went about to slay him. Which when the brethren knew, they brought him down to Caesarea, and*

sent him forth to Tarsus (Acts 9:26-30).

Paul himself reported later that God had also warned him in a trance to *"get thee quickly out of Jerusalem: for they will not receive thy testimony."* That was God at work for Saul's protection. So he fled to his former home in Tarsus, to testify there.

The enemies of Christ, embarrassed by Saul's conversion, had determined to stop his influence by killing him. But when he escaped out of their hands, the whole combination of events seemingly had a sobering effect upon their general attitude, which helped to ease the persecution.

> *Then had the churches rest throughout all Judaea and Galilee and Samaria, and were edified; and walking in the fear of the Lord, and in the comfort of the Holy Ghost, were multiplied (Acts 9:31).*

The Christians who were scattered by the persecution *"travelled as far as Phenice, and Cyprus, and Antioch, preaching the word to none but unto the Jews only."* But some from Cyprus and Cyrene, came to Antioch and *preached Christ to the Greeks.* *"And **the hand of the Lord was with them:** and a great number believed, and turned unto the Lord"* (Acts 11:19-21). The Gentile Christians at Antioch were open to a broader scope of evangelism than the Hebrew Christians at Jerusalem.

When the church at Jerusalem heard of the new awakening at Antioch, they sent Barnabas to encourage the believers. He was the right man for that assignment. Feeling the need for a man like Saul, he went to Tarsus and brought him to Antioch. For a whole year they labored there together, and taught much people. *"And the disciples were called Christians first at Antioch"* (Acts 11:26b).

Paul's First Missionary Journey

As the Gentile Christians at Antioch ministered to the Lord by prayer and fasting, **the Holy Spirit told them to set apart Barnabas and Saul** for the work to which God had called them. They commissioned them as missionaries and sent them abroad to evangelize Gentiles as well as Jews. Beginning with this first missionary journey, Saul became better known as Paul.

Although Paul was the Apostle of the Gentiles, his heartthrob always was, *"to the Jew first, and also to the Gentile."*[2] In every city he offered himself and the gospel first to the Jews, but he never overlooked the Gentiles. Jesus, as well as Paul, sought first the Jews,[3] and both laid down their lives for the Jews and the Gentiles.

Paul and Barnabas soon encountered Elymas the sorcerer, who withstood them. Satan always tries to resist the work of the Lord, but Satan is no match for the Holy Spirit. Paul set his eyes on Elymas and said,

> *O full of all subtilety and all mischief, thou child of the devil, thou enemy of all righteousness, wilt thou*

not cease to pervert the right ways of the Lord? And now, behold, the hand of the Lord is upon thee, and thou shalt be blind, not seeing the sun for a season. And immediately there fell on him a mist and a darkness; and he went about seeking some to lead him by the hand (Acts 13:10b, 11).

At Antioch in Pisidia, they were invited to preach in their synagogue. Paul preached Christ, by whom *"all that believe are justified from all things, from which ye could not be justified by the law of Moses."*[4] The next Sabbath almost the whole city came together to hear the Word.

*But when the Jews saw the multitudes, they were filled with envy, and spake against those things which were spoken by Paul, contradicting and blaspheming. Then Paul and Barnabas waxed bold, and said, It was necessary that **the word of God should first have been spoken to you**: but seeing ye put it from you, and judge yourselves unworthy of everlasting life, lo, we turn to the Gentiles (Acts 13:45, 46).*

Gentiles rejoiced and many believed, but the Jews stirred up persecution and expelled them out of their coasts (Acts 13:47-52). God seeks everyone, saves whosoever will, but forces no one.

In Iconium a great multitude of Jews and Greeks believed. *"But the unbelieving Jews stirred up the Gentiles, and made their minds evil affected against the brethren."* When there was an assault made to stone them, Paul and Barnabas fled to Lystra. There they preached the gospel[5] and healed an impotent man, lame from birth. Which, when the people saw, they could scarcely be restrained from sacrificing oxen unto the apostles. But after certain Jews from Antioch and Iconium had persuaded them, they stoned Paul and dragged him out of the city, supposing him to be dead (Acts 14:8-19).

> *Howbeit, as the disciples stood round about him, he rose up, and came into the city: and the next day he departed with Barnabas to Derbe (Acts 14:20).*

But after preaching the gospel at Derbe and evangelizing many people, they returned again to Lystra, Iconium and Antioch (the very places where Paul had been stoned and expelled), confirming and encouraging the souls of believers. When they had ordained elders in every church, they commended them to the Lord with prayer and fasting, and went back to their home base (Antioch in Syria), preaching the gospel as they went. *"And there they abode long time with the disciples"* (Acts 14:28).

During this interval at *home base*, Paul, Barnabas, Silas, and Titus attended the Jerusalem conference, where they all agreed that Gentiles may be fully accepted without being circumcised.

Paul's Second Missionary Journey

God had commissioned Paul as an apostle to the Gentiles, and the call to *missions* was in his blood. *"Paul said to Barnabas, Let us go again and visit our breth-*

ren . . . and see how they do." Barnabas determined to take his nephew, John Mark, along. Paul thought not so, and they disagreed strongly enough that they separated—an example of saintly men in human vessels.

John Mark, who was quite young, had gone along on their first journey, but soon, *"departing from them returned to Jerusalem"* (Acts 13:13). Paul feared Mark may give up again. Barnabas, uncle to John Mark, felt more lenient toward him, and may also have detected some growing maturity that Paul had not yet discovered. Later, Paul described Mark as *"profitable to me for the ministry"* (2 Timothy 4:11). Perhaps both were partly right and partly wrong.

This parting of ways resulted in two missionary teams. Barnabas took Mark, and sailed to Cyprus, and Paul chose Silas and went through Syria and Cilicia, confirming the churches. Then he came to Derbe and Lystra, where he found Timothy, a very dedicated young man.

Paul had taken Titus, an uncircumcised Greek, to the Jerusalem conference to help convince the Jews that physical circumcision is not essential for Gentiles. But Timothy he circumcised, not to improve Timothy's salvation, but to enhance his influence with the Jews, *"for they knew all that his father was a Greek"* (Acts 16:3). Paul, by precept and example, teaches us to pursue *"the things which make for peace, and things wherewith one may edify another"* (Romans 14:19).

*And as they went through the cities, they deliv-
ered them the decrees for to keep, that were ordained
of the apostles and elders which were at Jerusalem.
And so were the churches established in the faith, and
increased in number daily (Acts 16:4, 5).*

They *"were forbidden of the Holy Ghost to preach the
word in Asia,"* and the Spirit suffered them not to go
into Bithynia. By a vision in the night, Paul understood that Macedonia was where the Lord wanted
them to go (Acts 16:6-10). There they baptized Lydia
and her household, and delivered a slave girl from a
spirit of divination which had brought her masters
much gain by fortune telling. Sensitivity and loyal
obedience to the Holy Spirit is imperative to success-
ful ministry.

Paul and Silas suffered plenty for having delivered
the girl from demonic control. The multitude rose up
against them, rent off their clothes, beat them with
many stripes, and cast them into prison with their
feet fast in stocks. But God rewarded them with a
sanctified advertisement.

*At midnight Paul and Silas prayed, and sang
praises unto God: and the prisoners heard them. And
suddenly there was a great earthquake, so that the
foundations of the prison were shaken: and immediately all the doors were opened, and every one's bands
were loosed (Acts 16:25, 26).*

And he [the jailor] *took them the same hour of the
night, and washed their stripes; and was baptized, he*

and all his, straightway. And when he had brought them into his house, he set meat before them, and rejoiced, believing in God with all his house (16:33, 34).

Now they understood why the Lord sent them to Macedonia.

Another highlight for Paul was the city of Athens. His spirit was stirred, seeing Athens wholly given to idolatry. They even had one altar inscribed *"TO THE UNKNOWN GOD,"* just in case there may be one they hadn't heard of. Paul skillfully took advantage of that inscription, saying, *"This is the God I preach unto you."* Then he preached to them the true God as the Creator of all men, and Christ as the only Savior. When they heard of the resurrection from the dead, some mocked in unbelief. Others wanted to hear more, but few seemed fully convinced.

At Corinth, Jewish opposition was strong, but the chief ruler of the synagogue and many Corinthians, believed. Paul *"continued there a year and six months, teaching the word of God among them"* (Acts 18:9-11). From there, he went on through Ephesus, Caesarea, Jerusalem, and back to Antioch (Acts 18:18-22).

Paul's Third Missionary Journey

After revisiting the churches he had founded earlier, Paul came to Ephesus, where he found disciples who had been baptized unto John's baptism of repentance, but had not received the Holy Spirit. He instructed them more fully, and baptized them in the name of Jesus.

Paul separated the disciples from hardened unbelievers, and taught daily in the school of Tyrannus.

> *And this continued by the space of two years; so that all they which dwelt in Asia heard the word of the Lord Jesus, both Jews and Greeks. And God wrought special miracles by the hands of Paul: So that from his body were brought unto the sick handkerchiefs or aprons, and the diseases departed from them, and the evil spirits went out of them (Acts 19:10-12).*

Seven sons of a certain priest tried to cast out an evil spirit in the name of Jesus. The spirit answered, *"Jesus I know, and Paul I know; but who are ye?"* The man leaped on them and beat them severely. *"They fled out of that house naked and wounded. . . . Fear fell on them all, and the name of the Lord Jesus was magnified"* (Acts 19:13-17). Many who used curious arts brought their books, valued at fifty thousand pieces of silver, and burned them.

Demetrius, the silversmith who made shrines for the goddess Diana, instigated an uproar that ran wild. For two hours the rioters shouted, *"Great is Diana of the Ephesians."* The town clerk feared they may be challenged by their authorities for the uncontrolled uproar.[6] Paul called the disciples together, comforted them, and left for Greece, preaching, witnessing, and exhorting as he went. After three months in Greece,

Paul began his final return to Jerusalem.

During a midnight sermon at Troas, Eutychus, who was sitting in a window, went to sleep, *"fell down from the third loft, and was taken up dead."* Paul went down and embraced him, and his life was restored.

Paul's farewell words to the Ephesian elders who met him at Miletus[7] and his response to the prophet Agabus[8] who met him at Caesarea indicate his willingness to lay down his life for Christ who had died for him. His fearless commitment rang loud and clear:

> *What mean ye to weep and to break mine heart? for I am ready not to be bound only, but also to die at Jerusalem for the name of the Lord Jesus. And when he would not be persuaded, we ceased, saying, The will of the Lord be done (Acts 21:13b, 14).*

Paul, the Prisoner of the Lord

At Jerusalem, Paul was attacked by a mob of radicals, who would have killed him. But the chief captain and the Roman soldiers rushed upon them, took him out of their hands, and he was carried by the soldiers because of the violence of the people (Acts 21:35). Having obtained permission of the chief captain to speak to the people, Paul stood on the stairs and declared how God transformed him from a persecutor to an evangelist.

The Jews listened until Paul said how God sent him to preach to the Gentiles. Then they shouted, *"Away with such a fellow from the earth: for it is not fit that he should live"* (Acts 22:22). Only the fact that he was born as a Roman citizen saved him from scourging (Acts 22:24-29).

More than forty men had bound themselves under a curse to neither eat nor drink until they had killed Paul (Acts 23:12, 13). They either broke their vows or died of hunger and thirst. Paul had a promise from God that he would *"bear witness also at Rome,"*[9] which he did for at least two years.[10] Paul, in his own words, summarizes his sufferings for the Gospel's sake.

> . . . *in labours more abundant, in stripes above measure, in prisons more frequent, in deaths oft. Of the Jews five times received I forty stripes save one. Thrice was I beaten with rods, once was I stoned, thrice I suffered shipwreck, a night and a day I have been in the deep; In journeyings often, in perils of waters, in perils of robbers, in perils by mine own countrymen, in perils by the heathen, in perils in the city, in perils in the wilderness, in perils in the sea, in perils among false brethren; In weariness and painfulness, in watchings often, in hunger and thirst, in fastings often, in cold and nakedness (2 Corinthians 11:23b-27).*

Paul was a captive the last four years of his life: two years at Caesarea and two at Rome (Acts 23:23; 24:27; 28:30). Consequently, he never got to Spain physically, but the fruit of those years includes an extensive counseling ministry and four valuable epistles: Ephesians, Colossians, Philemon and Philippians. His many epistles continue to circle the earth.

Paul lived above his circumstances even in bondage. Philippians, though written in prison, is pleasantly seasoned with words like *"praise"* (twice), *"glory"* and *"joy"* (each 5 times), and *"rejoice"* (10 times). His death by martyrdom is not recorded in the Scriptures, but we have it from reliable sources that he was eventually beheaded at Rome.

The ultimate purpose of this chapter is the manifestation of God's power at work in a vessel of clay. Especially impressive is the transformation from a fiery enemy of Christ to one of the most fiery witnesses for Christ—purely a work of God. Are you and I as willing as Paul was to let God transform us, and to use us as He will, regardless of what it may cost us?

Questions for Consideration and Discussion

1. What qualified Saul to be chosen as an Apostle?
2. How was his conscience always "void of offence"?
3. Who really was it that brought Saul to Christ?
4. How soon and where did he seek divine counsel?
5. When and to whom did he go for human counsel?
6. Was he ever safe in Jerusalem after his conversion?
7. Who sought his life, his own people, or the Gentiles?
8. Who saved him from forty men who vowed to kill him?

202 God at Work in Saints of Old

9. Was civil incarceration his penalty or his protection?
10. What fruit do we have from his years in prison?

---

1. Acts 9:17, 18
2. Romans 2:9, 10; 1:16
3. Matthew 10:5, 6
4. Acts 13:16-41
5. Acts 14:1-7
6. Acts 19:24-41
7. Acts 20:25-38
8. Acts 21:10-13
9. Acts 23:11
10. Acts 28:14-31

18

Discipled by the Love of Jesus

Now there was leaning on Jesus' bosom,
one of his disciples, whom Jesus loved
(John 13:23).

John the Brother of James

John, the disciple, came on the scene as a young
man during the popularity of John the Baptist. To
distinguish him from the popular John, he sometimes
trailed in the shadow of his older brother, as *"John
the brother of James."*[1] With several Jameses in the com-
munity, James and John were identified as *"the sons
of Zebedee."*[2] Their mother was Salome,[3] claimed by
tradition to have been a sister to Jesus' mother. If
that is correct, then John was a first cousin to Jesus.
He was a disciple of John the Baptist before he knew
Jesus as the Messiah.

The name John occurs nineteen times in the Gospel of John, but it always refers to John the Baptist.
John the disciple's name never appears in his own
writings except in The Revelation. Five times he refers

to himself as the *other disciple,* three times as a disciple *whom Jesus loved,* and twice as *the elder* (2 John 1:1; 3 John 1:1). All of his writings were late in his life.

The Gospel of John starts out with a unique introduction of Jesus Christ, which we will discuss later. John the Baptist corrects some misconceptions about his own identity, and introduces Jesus to his audience as the **Lamb of God** and the **Son of God** (John 1:19-34).

> *Again the next day after John* [the Baptist] *stood, and two of his disciples; and looking upon Jesus as he walked, he saith, Behold the Lamb of God! And the two disciples heard him speak, and they followed Jesus (John 1:35-37).*

Jesus turned and saw them following, and asked, *"What seek ye."* They asked where He lived, and He invited them to *"come and see."* They went, and stayed with him that day.   One of the two was Andrew, Simon Peter's brother,[4] who first told his brother Simon. John doesn't name the other disciple, which is one evidence that it was John himself. Any of the others he would have named.

What they witnessed and experienced in Jesus' home that evening was undoubtedly a key factor in John's decision to be a disciple of Jesus. My guess is that before John went to bed that night, he had invited (if not convinced) his brother James to join them in their new discipleship.

Another evidence that John must have accompanied Andrew is that he writes like an eyewitness. How else would he remember nearly sixty years later what happened each day, and even that *"it was about the tenth hour"* when they came to Jesus' home and *"abode with him that day"*?

The next day Jesus found Philip, and Philip told Nathanael, of whom Jesus said, *"Behold an Israelite indeed, in whom there is no guile!"* Nathanael is the Bartholomew in the four lists of the twelve Apostles.

Being a *disciple* bears the thought of following as a *learner*. Jesus had a multitude of disciples who followed Him. From among them He chose twelve Apostles, whom He sent out to preach and teach. John became one of the most prominent Apostles, but in his writings he never identified himself as an Apostle.

John the Disciple Becomes an Apostle

*Now the names of the twelve apostles are these; The first, Simon, who is called Peter, and Andrew his brother; James the son of Zebedee, and **John** his brother; Philip, and Bartholomew; Thomas, and Matthew the publican; James the son of Alphaeus, and Lebbaeus, whose surname was Thaddaeus; Simon the Canaanite, and Judas Iscariot, who also betrayed him (Matthew 10:2-4).*

There are three other lists recording the names of the twelve apostles, including Mark 3:13-19, Luke

6:12-16, and Acts 1:13. In all four, Simon Peter heads the list, and **John** is either third or fourth, depending on whether Andrew follows his brother Simon or John. These two sets of brothers are always named first.

Their enthusiastic zeal for their Master undoubtedly contributed to their popularity. Since no mortal man is perfect in all his ways, even one's strengths can become his greatest weakness. Is that what happened to John when a Samaritan village refused to receive Jesus (Luke 9:51-56)? He and his brother James were so zealous for Jesus that they were ready *"to command fire to come down from heaven, and consume them, even as Elias did."*

Jesus rebuked them, and said, *"Ye know not what manner of spirit ye are of. For the Son of man is not come to destroy men's lives, but to save them."* Jesus, who *"knew what was in man,"* had probably sensed that problem in their nature before he surnamed them *"the sons of thunder"* (Mark 3:17). Being discipled by the love of Jesus, John's *thunder* became sanctified, and he obtained the unique distinction of being *"the disciple whom Jesus loved"*(John 20:2; 21:7, 20).

Jesus was no respecter of persons, but it is obvious that Peter, James, and John occasionally had intimate experiences with Jesus that the other apostles did not witness. They alone were with Him on the mount of transfiguration.[5] They saw His face *"shine as the sun,"* and His raiment so white *"as no fuller on earth can white them."* Twice we read that they alone saw Him raise the dead to life.[6] They were near, but slept, while Jesus wrestled for total surrender in Gethsemane.[7]

In some ways Peter and John were opposite personalities. Peter was probably the oldest of the Apostles, and John the youngest. Peter was bold, dominant, aggressive, commanding, blunt, and quick to speak. John was timid, unassuming, nonaggressive, subordinate, reserved, and slow to speak. Yet they were frequently singled out as a pair, and worked well together.

Jesus selected Peter and John to *"go and prepare us the passover, that we may eat"* (Luke 22:8). Later that same night, when Jesus was taken from Gethsemane to the high priest, *"Simon Peter followed Jesus, and so did **another disciple**,"* which, of course, was John. This time their roles were reversed. John went in with Jesus into the palace, but Peter, disoriented, stood outside the door. Then that *"other disciple"* went out and brought Peter in (John 18:15, 16). When Jesus was dying on the cross, John was the only apostle there, and Jesus consigned His mother into John's care. Peter must have been sorrowing elsewhere. On Resurrection morning, when Peter and John heard that the tomb was empty, they ran together to the tomb. By outrunning Peter, John got there first, but Peter was first to enter the tomb (John 20:2-8).

After Pentecost, Peter and John became an evangelistic team, preaching the resurrection of Jesus as they went. When people saw the boldness of Peter and John, they realized that they had been with Jesus (Acts 4:13). They were arrested, imprisoned, threatened, and forbidden to preach. But they said, *"We cannot but speak the things which we have seen and heard."* Later, they were sent to the city of Samaria, where, by their laying on of hands and praying, the Holy Spirit fell on Samaritan believers.

As the Holy Spirit worked in their individual personalities, their differences were blended into a unified, harmonious team. It was **God at Work in Saints of Old.**

The Gospel and Epistles of John

The Gospel of John is unique. He is silent about the birth, childhood, and youth of Jesus. He reveals more about Christ in eternity past, and in eternity future, than Matthew, Mark, and Luke combined. By the time of his writing he was probably the only surviving Apostle, and according to tradition he was the only one of the Twelve who died a natural death. God had preserved and was preparing John to write the final Revelation of Jesus Christ. John already appeared to be especially fitted for that assignment.

*He was in the world, and **the world was made by him**, and the world knew him not. He came unto his own, and his own received him not. But as many as received him, to them gave he power to become the sons of God, even to them that believe on his name: .*

. . And the Word was made flesh, and dwelt among us, (and we beheld his glory, the glory as of the only begotten of the Father,) full of grace and truth (John 1:10-12, 14).

John especially emphasized the deity of Jesus, who *"needed not that any should testify of man: for he knew what was in man."* He records the very vital teaching of Jesus on the new birth (John 3:3-7), and such sayings as, *"I am the way, the truth, and the life: no man cometh unto the Father, but by me." "He that hath seen me hath seen the Father." "Believest thou not that I am in the Father, and the Father in me? the words that I speak unto you I speak not of myself: but the Father that dwelleth in me, he doeth the works. Believe me that I am in the Father, and the Father in me"* (John 14:6b, 9b-11a).

John also clearly reveals the eternal preexistence of Christ in perfect union with the Father. It was John who wrote, *"No man hath seen God at any time."*[8] John records Jesus as saying, *"Not that any man hath seen the Father, save he which is of God, he hath seen the Father"* (John 6:46). Thereby, John indicates that Old Testament theophanies (visible appearances of God) were actually Christophanies (visible appearances of Christ). The preincarnate Christ was fully God, for *"the Word was God,"* and God was the Word.

The *disciple whom Jesus loved* was also an *Apostle of Love*. The word *love* appears twenty-two times in his Gospel and thirty-eight times in his first epistle. After spending three and a half years in intimate relationship with Jesus, followed by sixty years of walking with Him in the Spirit, He had accumulated a wealth of spiritual insight. His writings bubble over with the **life**, the **light**, and the **love** of Christ, the Son of God.

John wanted everyone to **know** Jesus. The word *know* occurs seventy-one times in the Gospel of John, and twenty-seven times in his first epistle. He speaks from his own intimate knowledge of and relationship with our Lord Jesus Christ: He said,

> *That which was from the beginning, which we have heard, which we have seen with our eyes, which we have looked upon, and our hands have handled, of the Word of life; (For the life was manifested, and we have seen it, and bear witness, and show unto you that eternal life, which was with the Father, and was manifested unto us;) That which we have seen and heard declare we unto you, that ye also may have fellowship with us: and truly our fellowship is with the Father, and with his Son Jesus Christ (1 John 1:1-3).*

> *These things have I written unto you that believe on the name of the Son of God;* **that ye may know that ye have eternal life**, *and that ye may believe on the name of the Son of God (1 John 5:13).*

The Revelation of Jesus Christ

John's most important role, no doubt, was his prophetic writing. He was exiled to the lonely Isle of Patmos, and divinely preserved to write The Revelation: God's last written message to mankind. It is not a book of fantasies, but one to be studied with awesome reverence and godly fear. God Himself calls it:

The Revelation of Jesus Christ, which God gave unto him, to show unto his servants things which must shortly come to pass; and he sent and signified it by his angel unto his servant John (Revelation 1:1).

Blessed is he that readeth, and they that hear the words of this prophecy, and keep those things which are written therein: for the time is at hand (Revelation 1:3).

Human manipulation is dangerous, but the Word itself is truth.

For I testify unto every man that heareth the words of the prophecy of this book, If any man shall add unto these things, God shall add unto him the plagues that are written in this book: And if any man shall take away from the words of the book of this prophecy, God shall take away his part out of the book of life, and out of the holy city, and from the things which are written in this book (Revelation 22:18, 19).

John saw Jesus coming as KING OF KINGS AND LORD OF LORDS to make final settlement with this Christ-denying, rebellious world. He saw the great white throne of judgment and the destiny of the wicked. *"Death and hell were cast into the lake of fire. . . . And whosoever was not found written in the book of life was cast into the lake of fire"* (Revelation 20:14, 15).

But, praise God, he also saw the destiny of the righteous: *"That great city, the holy Jerusalem, descending out of heaven from God, . . . And the city had no need of the sun, . . . for the glory of God did lighten it, and the Lamb is the light thereof, . . . And there shall in no wise enter into it any thing that defileth, . . . but they which are written in the Lamb's book of life"* (Revelation 21:10, 23, 27).

Is your name written there? Are you committed, by faith, to the Lord Jesus Christ, and walking with Him in joyful obedience to the Word of God? If not, I plead with you, to turn to Him immediately for pardon and cleansing. *"There is none righteous, no, not one: . . . For all have sinned, and come short of the glory of God"* (Romans 3:10b, 23). *"Neither is there salvation in any other: for there is none other name under heaven given among men, whereby we must be saved"* (Acts 4:12). Death seals your destiny forever! No one but Jesus can give you eternal life.

If you are walking with Jesus in joyful obedience to the Word of God, then God is at work in you today.

Questions for Consideration and Discussion

1. Whose disciple was John before he followed Jesus?
2. What convinced John that Jesus is the Messiah?
3. How did the chosen Apostles differ from disciples?
4. Who does the choosing that makes one a disciple?

5. What made Peter and John such good teammates?
6. How did their similarities and contrasts enhance their ministry?
7. What were some of John's greatest strengths?
8. What do you think was John's greatest assignment?
9. Who all was involved in their strife at the last supper?
10. What vital lesson are we to learn from that?

---

1. Matthew 10:2; Mark 3:17; 5:37
2. Matthew 26:37; Mark 10:35; Luke 5:10; John 21:2
3. Matthew 27:56; Mark 15:40
4. John 1:40
5. Matthew 17:1-8; Mark 9:2-10; Luke 9:28-36
6. Mark 5:37-43; Luke 8:51-54
7. Matthew 26:37-43; Mark 14:33-42
8. John 1:18; 1 John 4:12

You Can Find Our Books at These Stores:

GEORGIA
Montezuma
The Family Book Shop
912/472-5166

INDIANA
Lagrange
Pathway Bookstore
Wakarusa
Maranatha Christian Bookstore
219/862-4332

IOWA
Kalona
Friendship Bookstore

KENTUCKY
Harrodsburg
Kountry Kupboard
814/629-1588
Stephensport
Martin's Bookstore
270/547-4206

MARYLAND
Union Bridge
Home Ties
410/775-2511

MICHIGAN
Eveart
Hillview Books and Fabric
231/734-3394
Fremont
Helping Hand Home
231/924-0041

Snover
Country View Store
517/635-3764

MISSOURI
Rutledge
Zimmerman's Store
660/883-5766
St. Louis
The Homeschool Sampler
314/835-0863
Seymour
Byler Supply & Country Store
417/935-4522
Versailles
Excelsior Bookstore
573/378-1925

OHIO
Berlin
Gospel Book Store
Hopewell
Four Winds Bookstore
740/454-7990
Mesopotamia
Eli Miller's Leather Shop
440/693-4448
Middlefield
Wayside Merchandise Books
and Gifts
Millersburg
Country Furniture & Book-
store
330/893-4455

Plain City
Deeper Life Bookstore
614/873-1199

PENNSYLVANIA
Belleville
Yoder's Gospel Book Store
717/483-6697

Ephrata
Clay Book Store
717/733-7253

Conestoga Bookstore
717/354-0475

Guys Mills
Christian Learning
Resource
814/789-4769

Leola
Conestoga Valley Books
Bindery
717/656-8824

McVeytown
Penn Valley Christian Retreat
717/899-5000

Narvon
Springville Woodworks
856/875-6916

Springboro
Chupp's Country Cupboard
814/587-3678

Stoystown
Kountry Pantry
814/629-1588

TENNESSEE
Crossville
Troyer's Country Cupboard
931/277-5886

TEXAS
Kemp
Heritage Market and Bakery
903/498-3366

VIRGINIA
Dayton Farmer's Market
Books of Merit
540/879-5013

Harrisonburg
Christian Light
Publications
540/434-0768

Stuarts Draft
The Cheese Shop
540/337-4224

CANADA
British Columbia
Burns Lake
Wildwood Bibles and Books
250/698-7451

Ontario
Brunner
Country Cousins
519/595-4277

Order Form

To order, send this completed order form to:
**Vision Publishers, Inc.
P.O. Box 190
Harrisonburg, VA 22803
or fax
540-432-6530**

_____ _____
Name   Date

_____ _____
Mailing Address   Phone

_____
City   State   Zip

Seeing Christ in the Old Testament Quantity _____ x $8.99 each = _____

Seeing Christ in the Tabernacle Quantity _____ x $6.99 each = _____

God at Work in Saints of Old   Quantity _____ x $9.99 each = _____

Price _____

Virginia residents add 4.5% sales tax _____

Grand Total _____

All Prices Include Shipping and Handling

All Payments in US Dollars

☐ Check #_____
☐ Visa
☐ MasterCard

Card # ☐☐☐☐ ☐☐☐☐ ☐☐☐☐ ☐☐☐☐

Exp. Date ☐☐☐☐

Thank you for your order!

*For a complete listing of our books,
write for our catalog.*

Bookstore inquiries welcome

Order Form

To order, send this completed order form to:
Vision Publishers, Inc.
P.O. Box 190
Harrisonburg, VA 22803
or fax
540-432-6530

_____   _____
Name   Date

_____   _____
Mailing Address   Phone

_____
City   State   Zip

Seeing Christ in the Old Testament Quantity _____ x $8.99 each = _____

Seeing Christ in the Tabernacle   Quantity _____ x $6.99 each = _____

God at Work in Saints of Old   Quantity _____ x $9.99 each = _____

Price _____

Virginia residents add 4.5% sales tax _____

Grand Total _____

All Prices Include Shipping and Handling

All Payments in US Dollars

☐ Check #_____
☐ Visa
☐ MasterCard

Card # ☐☐☐☐ ☐☐☐☐ ☐☐☐☐ ☐☐☐☐

Exp. Date ☐☐☐☐

Thank you for your order!

*For a complete listing of our books,
write for our catalog.*

Bookstore inquiries welcome